LOST IRELAND

Dedication

This book is dedicated to my aunt, Maggie Fitzpatrick Khondoker (1945-2020), a proud Cavan woman, whose life in London touched and inspired many.

Acknowledgements

I would firstly like to thank Lisa Marie Griffith who generously put my name forward for this project. She is a great friend and scholar. Thanks to Frank Hopkinson of Pavilion Books who has shown enthusiasm and interest in the book and whose suggestions have greatly improved it.

The staff at the National Library of Ireland's Photographic Archive care for an outstanding collection of Irish photographs and those who work in the Rights and Reproduction section have always been especially helpful. I would like to thank my colleagues at the National Museum of Ireland particularly Brenda Malone and Alex Ward.

I am very grateful to my friends and family especially my nieces and nephew: Medb, Cormac and Doireann. My husband Niall McCormack has patiently advised and encouraged me throughout the compilation of this book and many other endeavours over the last twenty-five years.

Picture credits

The outstanding resources of the National Library of Ireland can be viewed at www.nli.ie or the National Library of Ireland on The Commons, www.flickr.com/photos/nlireland. Similarly the collections of the National Museums of Northern Ireland at www.nmni.com. All pictures in the book courtesy of the National Library of Ireland and from the Wiltshire Collection at the National Library of Ireland, with the following exceptions:
Alamy, pages 6, 7 (bottom), 9 (top), 11, 30, 31 (top), 37 (bottom), 39, 40, 42, 43, 48, 49, 51, 67 (bottom), 73, 75, 80, 81, 89 (right), 93, 95 (bottom), 111 (right), 116, 117, 118, 119 (bottom right), 136 (bottom right), 145, 149, 160 (bottom), 166, 167 (bottom right), 168 (right), 169, 171.
Cork Examiner, page 60.
Cork City Library, pages 26, 28, 29, 61.
County Wicklow Heritage, page 18.
Department of Community, Rural and Gaeltacht Affairs, page 64.
dúchas.ie / University College Dublin digitization project, pages 72, 74.
Dublin City Libraries, pages 123, 167 (left), 167 (top).
Getty Images, pages 9 (bottom), 31 (bottom left), 52 (right), 57 (top), 82, 85 (centre), 94, 95 (top), 106, 107 (top), 107 (bottom left), 109, 137, 158, 159, 165.
Library of Congress (LOC), pages 10, 33 (left), 36, 44, 46 (centre), 51 (centre), 59 (left), 65.
National Museums of Northern Ireland, pages 8, 11, 12 (top), 12 (bottom left and right), 20, 21, 24, 25, 58, 59 (right), 83, 91 (bottom left), 92, 96, 97, 98, 99 (top left and right), 112, 113, 119 (top), 119 (bottom left), 140, 141, 142, 143, 148, 153.
Musée Albert Kahn, page 57 (bottom).
Irish Independent, page 100.
Pavilion Image Library, pages 68 (bottom right), 69.
South Dublin County Library, pages 34, 35.
University College Dublin/Rex Roberts, pages 138, 139.

First published in the United Kingdom in 2021 by
PAVILION BOOKS
43 Great Ormond Street,
London WC1N 3HZ

© Pavilion Books 2021

ISBN: 978-1-911641-41-4

A CIP catalogue record for this book is available from the British Library.

10 9 8 7 6 5 4 3 2 1

Repro by Rival Colour Ltd, UK
Printed by 1010 Printing International Ltd, China

www.pavilionbooks.com

LOST IRELAND

Orla Fitzpatrick

PAVILION

CONTENTS

Moydrum Castle, Westmeath   p.38

Boyne Monument, Louth   p.44

Ballybunion Monorailway, Kerry   p.48

Slievemore Village, Achill Island, Mayo   p.72

Great Blasket Island, Kerry   p.80

Abbey Theatre, Dublin   p.94

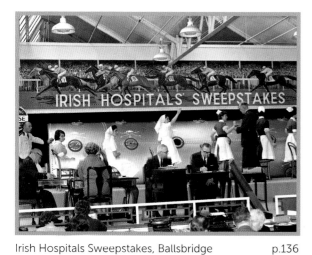

Irish Hospitals Sweepstakes, Ballsbridge   p.136

Phoenix Park Racecourse, Dublin   p.144

Ferbane Power Station, Offaly   p.160

INTRODUCTION

Ireland's architectural heritage is perhaps best known through its rural thatched cottages and romantic medieval castles. Its Victorian streetscapes, industrial complexes and lavish entertainment venues were not considered as typically Irish and therefore their eradication through neglect or ignorance has often been overlooked by historians and conservationists. Ireland escaped the aerial bombardment and destruction of the Second World War (with the exception of the Belfast Blitz of April 1941) nonetheless its revolutionary period, which included the Easter Rising of 1916 and the subsequent War of Independence (1919-1921) and Civil War (1922-1923), impacted upon city and townscape, flattening commercial properties and vernacular buildings alike. Prior to this the country's place within the British Empire and its system of landownership, generated wealth and its attendant infrastructure and buildings. These took the form of landmark buildings such as Dublin's Custom House designed by James Gandon and the Georgian townhouses and the 'Big Houses' built on

BELOW Mitchelstown in County Cork suffered its fair share of evictions during the Plan of Campaign in the 1880s, when tenants refused to pay the rents demanded. Occupants resisted the landowners and their agents by boarding up doors and inserting thorn bushes in the windows.

estates throughout the Irish countryside. The loss of many of these buildings is integral to understanding the country's post-colonial status and its complex history. The 'Lost Ireland' depicted in this book offers a way of exploring many strands of Irish history. These range from the vanished linen factories and shipyards of the North's industrial heartland to the statues and monuments associated with the British Empire which were removed or blown-up in a dramatic fashion over the centuries.

Many of the images in this book were sourced from the Victorian firm of William Lawrence whose topographical views of cities, towns and landmarks, captured the country in the decades prior to independence. These views were taken by the photographer Robert French and are rich in detail and atmosphere. The business operated out of O'Connell Street, Dublin's main thoroughfare, where the family ran a fancy goods, toy and photographic portrait studio. Whilst the Lawrence collection covers the entire island of Ireland, many of the Northern Irish photos in this book were taken by Robert John Welch. His work depicting Belfast's industrial heritage reveals the scale of the shipyards where the *Titanic* was built and a linen industry which boasted the largest spinning mill in the world. Both counter notions of Ireland as solely rural and agricultural.

Ireland's urban architecture in the form of its Georgian townhouses represents an aspect of the built environment which was ravaged through either poverty, neglect or thoughtless development. Many of these once grand residences, which were decorated by the finest of Irish and Italian craftsmen, became tenements following the Act of Union in 1800 which saw the end of the Irish parliament in Dublin and Ireland's incorporation within the United Kingdom. During the 1960s, developers were keen to replace these unbroken Georgian streetscapes with pastiche copies of the originals or large-scale office blocks in a derivative modernism. Some of the remaining Georgian Squares are now recognised for the grandeur that they give to the city's centre, however, others such as those located on the northside's Mountjoy Square languish in near dereliction.

An important presence in the Irish landscape, were the 'Big Houses' owned by the Anglo-Irish ascendancy upon whose estates the majority of Irish people were tenants. These 'worlds within worlds' reflected the wealth and taste of their owners ranging in style

from Medieval tower house to Palladian or Gothic-revival mansions. The landowners often spent beyond their means expressing their creativity, whimsy, and playfulness in collaboration with the notable architects of their period. Follies, gate lodges, landscaped gardens and cottage ornés were also built on these estates and these smaller constructions often outlasted the main 'Big House.' The breaking up of many of these estates and the transfer of land ownership in the decades before and after independence left many of these big

ABOVE The seafront at Bray during the Bray Regatta some time in the 1930s. Bray is featured in the book for its lost Martello Tower, the grand Marine and International hotels, Dr. Barter's elegant Moorish Baths and the Ladies Public Baths, from the roof of which this photo was taken.

RIGHT The Ballybunion Monorailway was a pioneering rail system devised by a French engineer, Charles Lartigue. It ran between Ballybunion and Listowel, but closed in 1924.

house owners marooned without a role. Some houses were burned during the War of Independence (1919-1921) or the Civil War (1922-1923) where they were seen as symbols of an external power and injustice (despite that fact that many of the families were resident in Ireland for centuries). Other houses were abandoned and slowly dissolved into the landscape and the loss of the fine examples of Irish craftsmanship that they contained is to be lamented.

The revolutionary period, during which Ireland fought for independence from Britain, and its resulting civil war wreaked havoc on prime examples of Irish architecture and the capital city's main thoroughfare Sackville/O'Connell Street. The 1916 Rising left the city centre in ruin and resulted in the loss of the General Post Office and many of the most novel and interesting commercial buildings in the city, for example, Clerys

department store and the Dublin Bread Company. The Public Record Office in the Four Courts was destroyed during the Civil War, taking with it much of Ireland's historic past including census records and irreplaceable manuscript materials. Both the General Post Office and the Four Courts were rebuilt in the early years of the independent Irish State.

Typical of most Victorian administrations, incarceration and institutional care generated large-scale buildings which dominated the landscape of most major towns: mental asylums, orphanages, prisons, industrial schools and Magdalene laundries for unmarried mothers can be included in this. All speak of a dark aspect of the nation's history.

As care switched towards a community setting from the 1980s many of these imposing structures became derelict as their unwieldy size and layout

made then unsuitable for other uses.

Entertainment venues represented glamour and escape and these sites were some of the most lavish and fanciful buildings to be built in the late nineteenth and twentieth century Ireland. Theatres such at the Ritz in Belfast and the Art Deco dream palaces that housed cinemas fell into abeyance as the public's tastes shifted towards home entertainment and television and video rather than music hall and movies. In Northern Ireland, the troubles seriously impacted upon the social life of its cities. Amid curfews, searches and bomb threats, people were less likely to venture into cinemas and thus many of John McBride Neill's landmark Art Deco cinemas closed and were converted to other uses, or demolished.

Monuments have always been the focal point for protest and symbols of British rule bore the brunt of this anger culminating most spectacularly in the destruction of Nelson's Pillar on Dublin's O'Connell Street, which was dramatically blown up in 1966. Less spectacular but equally ignominious was the removal of the statue of Queen Victoria which was shifted from its original location on Leinster Lawn to various locations around Dublin before eventual shipment to Australia where it now stands in front of a shopping centre in Sydney. Other monuments which were eliminated include the Boyne Obelisk and the statue of King William of Orange, both of which feature in this book.

Just as much of Ireland's built heritage has been lost due to uneven economic development and a lack of wealth, economic 'good times' and booms have also instigated the removal of much that was of architectural worth. The 'Celtic Tiger' of the mid 1990s to the early 2000s and its resultant housing boom saw the replacement of many sites of leisure

BUNDLING YORK STREET MILL BELFAST.

R.W.1231.

LEFT The York Street Spinning Mill in Belfast was at one time Ireland's largest linen producer with a number of specialist rooms all contributing to the process.

OPPOSITE PAGE TOP The Blasket Islands could be cut off from the mainland for days, and so the decision was taken to abandon Great Blasket in 1953. Gearóid Cheaist Ó Catháin was the only child on the island from 1951 to 1953.

OPPOSITE PAGE BOTTOM King George II, King William III and Queen Victoria all had prominent statues removed after Ireland gained its independence from Britain, but Admiral Nelson continued to gaze down O'Connell Street until the 1960s.

to make way for apartment complexes and housing estates. A notable loss for Dublin was the Phoenix Park racecourse. Hastily constructed factories and housing complexes often replaced vernacular buildings which were seldom listed as protected structures. Likewise much of the elaborate street furniture which gives an urban landscape its individual character was lost during this period.

There are perhaps surprisingly few public houses in this book. Whilst many have been demolished most remain having modernised or adapted to accommodate a changing clientele: be it lounge bars for women from the 1960s onwards to the restaurants and gastro pubs of the 2000s. Of those that were lost, their interiors were unfortunately seldom photographed and many had similar exteriors. One exception is the Irish House in Dublin whose elaborate facade of stucco work is featured within this book. This lost gem was adorned with figures and motifs relating to the Irish history. It was demolished to make way for Sam Stephenson's bunker-like offices for Dublin City Corporation's headquarters. In many ways, this epitomises the wanton destruction of Dublin which was enacted from the 1960s and which saw the city lose much of its local character and colour. Indeed the association of Ireland with the rural has resulted in a somewhat hostile and aggressive disregard for the country's urban architecture and heritage.

This book deviates from more obvious choices to include the vernacular and the industrial. It also showcases lost, fanciful and fun buildings and the many fads, fashions and trends which were embraced by the country's builders and architects. These range from Moorish baths in Victorian Bray to the Art Deco splendour of the Aspro Factory. Their loss and study can perhaps guide us towards what is worthy of preservation from our current architectural inventory.

Orla Fitzpatrick,
July 2020

DUNLUCE CASTLE, COUNTY ANTRIM
ABANDONED 1690s

Dunluce Castle is a medieval stronghold situated on the coast of Antrim. Perched on a highly defensible promontory and only accessible via a bridge, it was built around 1500 by the McQuillan clan who emigrated to Ireland from Scotland. Despite its strong position, the castle was seized by Sorley Boy MacDonnell (from Islay) following the Battle of Orla in 1565.

While its location had strategic benefits and prevented it from sustained attack over the years, it resulted in several parts of the building falling into the sea. Legend has it that a portion of the kitchen fell into the water below and that only the kitchen boy who was sitting in a corner of the room survived. It's a good story, but much of the kitchen remains intact with the oven and fireplace remaining visible. In the 18th century another portion fell into the sea – this time the North Wall.

Recent archaeological excavations have revealed the remains of a town that was built around the castle. It had cobbled streets and an estimated population of three hundred. Finds at the site have included a 16th-century Polish coin, which is viewed as evidence of the trade between Scottish merchants and Poland. There were also coins from the days of Elizabeth I and Charles I. The town, which dated from around 1608, was destroyed several decades later.

The outcome of the Battle of the Boyne in 1690 was pivotal to the fortunes of the castle and the MacDonnell family as they took the side of the defeated King James II. Impoverished after the battle, they abandoned the castle in the 1690s.

From the Victorian era it was a much-visited romantic ruin, not far from the spectacular basalt columns of the Giant's Causeway. The castle has featured on several record covers, most notably on the inner sleeve of Led Zeppelin's 1973 album *Houses*

OPPOSITE PAGE Dunluce Castle is perched high on basalt cliffs. Twenty-five metres (82 feet) below is the spectacular Mermaid's Cave from which Maeve Roe is said to have embarked on her final fatal journey.

BELOW LEFT Sorley Boy MacDonnell is said to have salvaged cannon from a wrecked Spanish Armada galleon and installed them in the towers.

BELOW The entrance bridge to the castle photographed in the early 20th century.

of the Holy. The album's front cover, also featured the nearby Causeway.

Naturally the castle has a ghost story or two. Maeve Roe, the only daughter of Lord McQuillan, was said to have been imprisoned by her father in a tower at the castle. In a tale reminiscent of Romeo and Juliet she had fallen in love with the son of a neighbouring, feuding clan. The young lovers escaped but were drowned, and her wails can be heard around the castle.

In recent years, the castle has featured in the hit HBO series *Game of Thrones*, where it was known as the Pyke stronghold, seat of the House of Greyjoy, rulers of the Iron Islands. The dramatic setting perfectly matches the mood of the series and, along with locations such as Carrick-a-Rede rope bridge and the Dark Hedges avenue, has done much to put Northern Ireland back on the international tourism market.

Some also believe that the castle was the inspiration for the castle of Cair Paravel in C. S. Lewis' *The Chronicles of Narnia*. Lewis, who was born in Belfast in 1898, maintained his connections with Ireland despite living in England from the age of nine.

LEFT The Giant's Causeway Tramway, the world's first hydro-electric powered railway, ran from Portrush Station, past Dunluce, through Bushmills to the Giant's Causeway. Nine miles (15 kilometres) long, it opened in 1883 and was eventually replaced by a bus after the 1949 season.

OPPOSITE PAGE Today, Dunluce Castle is an essential stop on any *Game of Thrones* tour of Northern Ireland.

BELOW Tourists take history notes in the 1930s.

PLAN OF CAMPAIGN EVICTIONS, COUNTY CLARE

1880s

Widespread evictions took place during a period of the Land War known as the Plan of Campaign. Tenants of cottages and smallholdings felt they had been exploited by (often absent) landlords and their agents. Instead of paying the rent demanded, they offered what they considered to be a fair rent to landlords. If these revised rents were refused the tenants then withheld all payments and the monies were centrally pooled and redistributed to aid those who had been evicted. The campaign was organized by the Irish National League and its leaders, including William O'Brien, John Dillon and Timothy Harrington. These two photographs show an eviction which took place on the Vandeleur Estate in County Clare in July 1888. The cottage shown in the image was the home of T. Birmingham, who rented it from the Estate.

The images were taken by the firm of William Lawrence, whose photographer traversed the country, mainly taking landscape images or street views that were in turn sold through their shop on Sackville (later

OPPOSITE PAGE Tenants took to filling doors and windows with thorn bushes and brushwood to resist eviction. Hot water and cow dung were also used to repel landowners' agents who had to resort to a battering ram to gain entry.

BELOW The Vandeleur Estate evictions were well documented by the William Lawrence company (WL on photos) often with both sides of the argument willing to pose for the camera.

BATTERING RAM . 1769 . W.L.

EVICTION SCENE. 1767. W.L.

O'Connell) Street. The campaigns were often directed towards absentee landlords who were based in England but who took little interest in their Irish estates. The Lawrence Collection contains sixty eviction scenes which were most likely taken by their main photographer Robert French. It is difficult to discern the exact political leanings of William Lawrence; however, he was an astute businessman who knew that there was an appetite for topical and nationalist subjects. French's images were sold as lantern slides and used by supporters of the Land League in lectures and talks. There were an estimated 70,000 evictions recorded from 1849 to the late 1880s. These images were also reproduced in newspapers sympathetic to the tenants' plight and, in addition to the tenants, featured the Royal Irish Constabulary, local officials and the landowners.

There has been much debate as to the staged nature of the images and, indeed, they are not the action shots of later photojournalism. Rather, those shown were posed and directed by the photographer, who arrived during or after the eviction but due to technological restrictions was confined to photographing a kind of re-enactment of the event that had recently happened. Battering rams often appear in the images and the damage that resulted from their use is vividly shown. This destruction was viewed as a means of deterring the families from re-occupying the homestead. In latter decades these destroyed and broken-down cottages are often mislabelled or shown out of context as examples of the poor standard of housing. Taking photographs across the country, French did record the names of the families shown, and these specifics added to the power of the images.

Also shown (right) are the Land League huts which were the temporary constructions used to house those who had been evicted. They were built to a uniform plan and the scheme was administered by the Ladies Land League. Although temporary and difficult to heat they represented an ingenious albeit short-term solution for those who were made homeless through eviction.

OPPOSITE PAGE The staged photograph of the eviction of Thomas Considine at Moyasta, County Clare.

MARTELLO TOWERS
DEMOLISHED IN BRAY, 1884

These rounded defensive towers were erected throughout Britain and Ireland in the early 19th century. They were built to thwart a French invasion during the Napoleonic Wars and were located strategically along the coast. Fifty were built in Ireland between 1804 and 1817. The towers' design, which was inspired by earlier examples in Corsica, included thickly built walls – some up to 9 feet (2.7 metres) thick – and flat roofs upon which cannon were mounted. Martello towers were often built within sight of each other in order to allow for communication between them and to warn of any approaching threat. Most of the towers had an 18-pounder gun, and artillery batteries were usually located close to the towers; some of these remain intact.

The majority of the Irish towers were located close to Dublin, with twelve to the north of the city and sixteen on the south coast. Of the twenty-eight located near the capital, twenty-one are still standing, although not all are well preserved. For example, the tower in the coastal town of Balbriggan in North County Dublin is missing its top and in a dilapidated state.

James Joyce set the opening scene of his novel *Ulysses* in a Martello tower in Sandycove, County Dublin. This was a tower in which he had briefly stayed as the guest of the writer Oliver St. John Gogarty in 1904. Gogarty was the inspiration for the character Malachi 'Buck' Mulligan. The tower was bought by the modernist architect Michael Scott (who redesigned the Abbey Theatre) in 1954 and it is now a museum celebrating Joyce's literature. The tower plays an integral role in the annual Bloomsday celebrations which take place on the 16th of June, the date on which *Ulysses* is set.

The surviving towers have been put to a variety of uses. Some of the remaining towers are in private ownership while others have been used as museums or heritage centres; for example, the tower in Howth in north County Dublin, now houses the Hurdy Gurdy Museum of Vintage Radio. The Martello tower at Seapoint, County Dublin, is occasionally open for tours, while the Sandymount tower was converted for restaurant use but has remained empty for thirty years or so.

However, a number of the towers have been lost over the years – some to inexorable coastal erosion, such as the one located at Corke Abbey, County Wicklow, which fell into the sea. Only one of the three Bray Martello towers remains. The third (above), which had been damaged by high seas in 1878, was demolished in 1884. This was to make way for the Grand Marine Promenade, which stretched for 2 miles (3 kilometres) and provided a walkway for tourists, protecting them from the sea. Two towers in the Dublin area were demolished in the 1860s to make way for railway lines.

ABOVE After two failed attempts by the French to invade Ireland in 1796 and 1798 a series of Martello towers were built including this one at Bray, removed in 1884.

OPPOSITE PAGE Howth Martello tower overlooking Dublin Bay photographed in the late 19th century. It survives today and has been repurposed as a radio museum.

CEREMONIAL ARCHES, BELFAST

REMOVED 1885

The royal visit of the Prince and Princess of Wales to Ulster in 1885 gave their loyal subjects an opportunity to express support and their belief in the union of Ireland with Britain. The erection of ceremonial arches was one way in which this was manifested on the Belfast streetscape. The erection of triumphal arches in Northern Ireland is not reserved for royal visits; it is a tradition which persists into the 21st century, where the loyalist community, in order to demarcate their territory, adorn traditional marching routes with them. Typically these arches are decorated with floral displays (incorporating orange lilies and evergreen leaves) and are topped with images of King William III of Orange.

The royal couple's itinerary in 1885 brought them to locations that emphasized Northern Ireland's industrial successes and loyalty to the crown. Visits to linen factories and institutions which identified with loyalist concerns formed much of the tour. The couple

and their son, Prince Albert Edward, arrived by Royal steamer on the 18th of June; however, newspaper reports show that the weather was not good for their first day. They visited the York Street Spinning Mill, one of the largest mills in the world, where they were presented with embroidered handkerchiefs. This was followed by luncheon at the Town Hall and then a visit to another Belfast industry: the firm of Marcus Ward and Co., the printers and publishers who specialized in children's books and greeting cards. They then proceeded to Queen's University and the Botanic Gardens. At the latter location 20,000 children were arranged in line to greet them, while the students at the college held a torchlit procession. They then travelled from Belfast to Derry via train.

It should be borne in mind that tensions were running high in the country due to continued agitation for tenants' rights by the Land League. Indeed, three thousand protesters turned out in Cork and the royal

couple were hissed and jeered.

The arches mirrored the sentiments of the loyalist community in Belfast and made an impactful and striking presence on the streets. One of the arches represented the trades of Belfast and was emblazoned with mottoes such as 'Trade is the golden girdle of the globe' and 'Employment is nature's physician'.

It was reported that some of the decorations were damaged by the bad weather and the temporary arches were removed after the royal entourage left.

OPPOSITE PAGE AND LEFT Two views of the elaborate Trades Arch – with a spinning wheel prominent – outside White Linen Hall.

ABOVE The Victoria Street Arch with its simple Welcome message.

NEW TIPPERARY, COUNTY TIPPERARY
DEMOLISHED 1892

In 1888–89, the residents of Tipperary town were in dispute with a local landlord over rents. This was during the height of the Land War when tenants around Ireland sought to attain fixity of tenure, fair rents and the right to purchase lands. It was known as the Plan of Campaign, a mass movement which employed peaceful methods of protest such as boycotting, withholding of rent and mass meetings. However, there was also some violence targeted at landlords and their agents. The landlord for properties in Tipperary town was Arthur Smith-Barry (one of County Cork's two members of Parliament), and Tipperary town tenants, in solidarity with those in Cork, decided to withhold rents. Some were evicted and it was decided to build new streets on the western outskirts of the town on land that was not owned by Barry. Funds were raised for the construction of 'New Tipperary' through the wider Land League organization, and monies came from the Irish diaspora in America and Australia.

Robert Gill was the architect of the new development. One of the streets contained twenty-three small houses and nine shops, while Parnell Street had thirteen shops. The bulk of the money was spent on the glass-roofed arcade. The official opening of the William Smith Arcade on the 12th of April, 1890, was a grand affair with 600 guests in attendance, and it attracted much media attention. The arcade had a long glass roof and the building was divided into twelve stalls or units. Forty shopkeepers left the Old Town, and at its peak two newspapers were issued from New Tipperary.

The experiment was short-lived and it was reported that many of the businesses had moved back to Old Tipperary by 1892. Newspapers of the time cite the lack of public houses as part of the problem, as no alcohol licences were granted for that part of the town. One of the main instigators of the project was Father David Humphreys, who was supported by national leaders, including John Dillon and William O'Brien. Many felt, however, that in the end the local Tipperary people were let down and abandoned, and had been duped into becoming involved in the campaign. Others maintain that Smith-Barry, the landlord at the centre of the dispute, was relatively fair to his tenants. Funds

from central headquarters dried up when the leaders absconded to America under threat of arrest. There was also fallout from a split in the Parliamentary Party (the leading nationalist party), the result of its leader Charles Stuart Parnell's affair with Kitty O'Shea. While New Tipperary ultimately failed, the endeavour was a brave collective attempt which challenged the power of landlords.

In the end, many of the tenants settled with the landlord and returned to Old Tipperary. The arcade was demolished on the 11th of August, 1892. Some of the timber-constructed houses remain and the streets were eventually absorbed into Old Tipperary.

OPPOSITE PAGE AND ABOVE The funds to build New Tipperary and its impressive commercial arcade were raised in Australia and America. Though short lived, it forced the hand of the "rackrenting landlord".

ARCADE. NEW TIPPERARY. 2571. W.L.

LINEN HALL BELFAST. RW. 27.

WHITE LINEN HALL, DONEGALL SQUARE, BELFAST
DEMOLISHED 1896

The size and scale of the White Linen Hall in Belfast reflected the importance of that industry to the city and Ulster's economy. Constructed between 1783 and 1784, its purpose was to facilitate the sale of bleached linens and to regulate prices. It was financed by subscriptions and demonstrated the growing autonomy and industrial muscle of Belfast's linen merchants. Another linen hall had been built in Newry, County Down, during the same period; however, it was the Belfast one which took prominence over both the Newry and Dublin halls.

The architect was most likely Roger Mulholland. Other buildings designed by Mulholland included the First Presbyterian Church on Rosemary Street, Belfast, and St. Anne's Vicarage on Donegall Street. Plans reveal that it was intended that a canal would pass in front of the Linen Hall building in order to facilitate easy transportation of goods from the exchange, but this was never built.

Constructed on four acres of land granted by the Earl of Donegall, the scale of the building was immense and it was reported that it once housed a table around which 354 people could gather. It included a large quadrangle and multiple offices and rooms where linen goods were displayed and stamped with the maker's name before export. In addition to the construction of the Linen Hall, new modern streets (now Donegall Square and Donegall Place) were built and the entire complex has had a lasting impact upon the city's streetscape and layout.

A subscription library previously called the Belfast Reading Society and the Belfast Society for Promoting Knowledge, moved into the White Linen Hall building in 1802. Now known as the Linen Hall Library it is the oldest library in Belfast. Some of the early founders of the library became involved in the radical politics of the 1790s. Its second librarian, Thomas Russell, was a member of the United Irishmen, a liberal group

formed in Belfast who went on to instigate the 1798 rebellion. Between 1792 and 1833 the library also housed a museum and reading rooms, where the latest pamphlets and newspapers could be consulted. The library moved from the Linen Hall in 1888 to a location at nearby Donegall Square in which it has remained. Its highlights include books printed in Belfast, early newspapers and political pamphlets, and a strong theatre and performing arts collection.

Queen Victoria awarded Belfast city status in 1888 and from then on plans were made to build a city hall to match this elevated status. The decision to demolish the Linen Hall was a controversial one and divided politicians upon Nationalist/Unionist lines, with the former finding symbolic value in a building which had direct links to the rebellion of 1798. This international linen exchange was demolished in 1896 to make way for Belfast's City Hall which opened a decade later in 1906.

ABOVE The Linen Hall Library is the oldest library in Belfast. It survived despite the loss of its host building and is now based in an old linen warehouse in Donegall Square.

OPPOSITE PAGE Donegall Square is now at the heart of Belfast's Linen Quarter.

LEFT Sometimes known as Old Linen Hall, the Georgian buildings were demolished to make way for the far grander Belfast City Hall.

after they took their life in their hands on the chute, visitors could hire gondolas and swan boats.

The chute was built on the River Lee, close to the Industrial Hall, and cost £3,000. It was not ready in time for the opening day on the 1st of May, 1902, but instead opened one week later. Cars gradually climbed to a height of 70 feet (21 metres) to reach the top of the chute. A newspaper account from November 1903, refers to an accident that occurred on the water chute when a young woman was thrown out of the boat; however, she was rescued uninjured.

The chute proved to be one of the most popular thrill-rides at the exhibition and a similar attraction was installed at the Irish International Exhibition, which took place in Herbert Park, Ballsbridge, in 1907. Called the Canadian Water Chute, it made a profit of £7,000, which was a considerable amount of money at the time. This event attracted almost three million visitors, which indicates the pull that such spectacles had for the Edwardian public.

A pedestrian bridge dating from 1927, known as Daly's Bridge, now spans the Lee at the same location as the water chute. All the buildings were dismantled when the exhibition finally closed on the 31st of October 1903.

The Cork International Exhibition took place in an area called the Mardyke in Cork City between 1902 and 1903. The world's first industrial exhibition, the Great Exhibition of the Works of Industry of All Nations, had occurred in London in 1851 and it spawned many similar events over the next decades. The organizers intended to showcase innovation and industry as well as provide entertainment and novelty for the general population. Water chutes became a regular feature at such exhibitions.

Cork City had held Ireland's first industrial exhibition in 1852; however, it was a relatively small affair compared to the subsequent exhibitions that took place later in the century and Cork's second

exhibition of 1902/03. The 44-acre (17-hectare) site, now Fitzgerald's Park, was located on reclaimed land. Over a million people visited the event which was open between spring and summer 1902 and then reopened the following spring/summer of 1903. It included several dedicated buildings and pavilions showcasing Irish manufacturers and art as well as goods from around the world. There were several restaurants (including a temperance restaurant and a creamery), a shooting gallery and a skating rink.

The switchback railway, a precursor to the rollercoaster, was a big success for those seeking thrills similar to the water chute. The organizers made the most of the exhibition's waterside location and,

OPPOSITE PAGE Shoot the Chute rides were pioneered in the United States in 1884 by J. P. Newburg. They consisted of flat-bottomed boats winched by a cable to the top of a ramp and let go. Usually splashing down in a small enclosed lagoon, the River Lee was a far more challenging place to recover the boats from.

ABOVE LEFT A distant view along the River Lee to the Water Chute with the more genteel form of recreation – rowing skiffs – in the foreground.

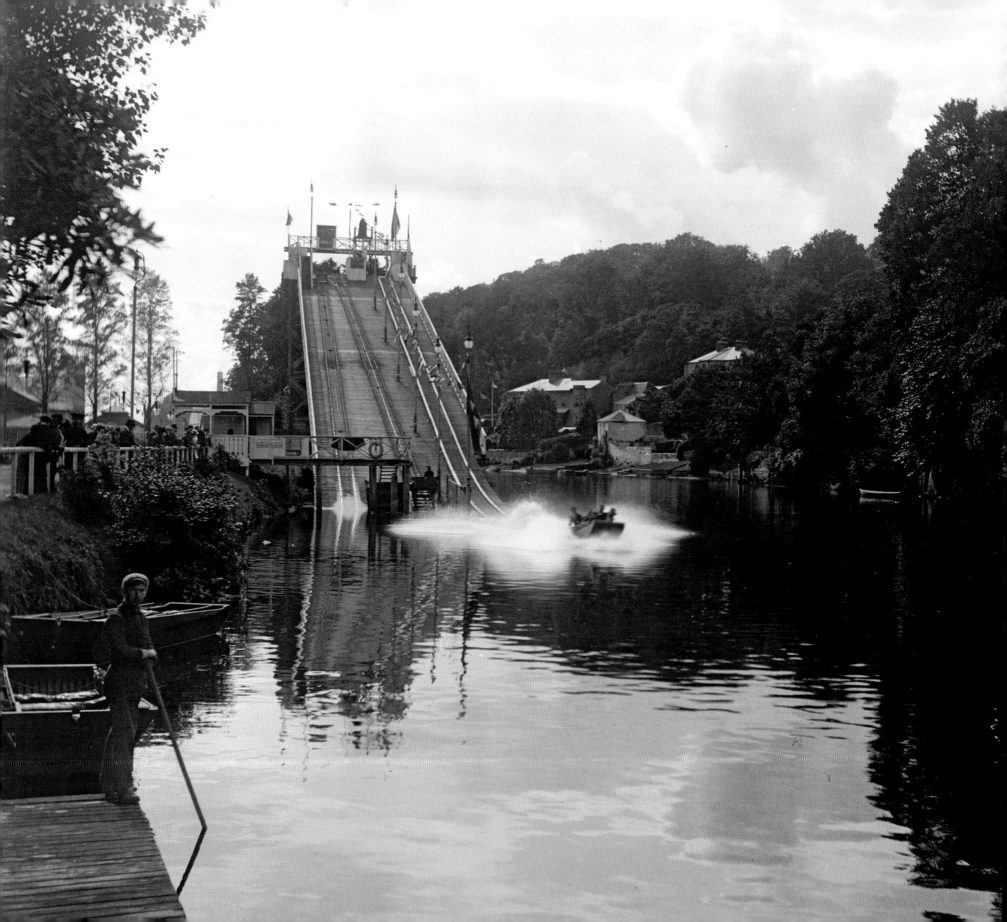

INTERNATIONAL EXHIBITION, CORK

DISMANTLED 1903

The 1902/03 Cork International Exhibition was one of the most successful industrial exhibitions ever held in Ireland. It showcased products from all over Ireland and the world. All the main buildings were designed by Henry A. Cutler and the architect William O'Connell. Cutler was also the city surveyor responsible for civic works such as the Cork City Swimming Baths. Another Cork architect, Arthur Hill, was responsible for the Canadian pavilion, the Fine Arts & Archaeological Hall, the President's Pavilion and the central bandstand.

The Industrial Hall was the largest building on the site and it had seven parallel avenues: three on each side of a main thoroughfare. It had a Corinthian portico and the main steps were made of Irish cut stone. The Women's Section highlighted the work undertaken in convents, and cottage industries such as lacemaking.

The Department of Agriculture and Technical Instruction also had a space within the hall and they put on regular demonstrations of small-scale industrial and agricultural processes such as churning. The entrance to the Department's section was decorated with Celtic pillars made of plaster mimicking Cormac's Chapel in Cashel, and the exhibition organizers made much of the fact that the decorations and pillars within the hall were made of 'fibrous plaster'.

Other industries that were showcased included Donegal carpets, Waterford glass, Blarney wools, Belleek pottery and Bushmills whiskey. The Japanese, Italian, and Austrian displays were also found within the Industrial Pavilion.

One of the most novel stands in the Industrial Building was that constructed by the Dublin and Belfast umbrella manufacturer Henry Johnston, which was a replica of Blarney Castle made entirely out of blackthorn sticks. Musical performances included two visits by Herr Julian Kandt's Viennese orchestra.

On the 31st of October 1903, the day of the exhibition's closure, newspaper notices announced the sale of the exhibition fixtures and fittings and these included 2,000 garden chairs, 2,500 bow-back Windsor chairs and several thousand sheets of glass in various sizes. The final night of the exhibition was marked by a ball and concert with music by the Cork Workingmen's Band. A fireworks display took place over the exhibition grounds.

Almost all the exhibition buildings were demolished soon after it closed and the grounds were handed over to Cork Corporation for use by the public. There is one significant legacy: the Cork Public Museum is located in the park in a building which was known as the Shrubberies during the 1902 exhibition.

OPPOSITE PAGE, LEFT AND BELOW The International Exhibition of 1902/1903 was a far grander affair than its 1852 predecessor, with a Canadian Pavilion, art gallery, machinery hall and industrial hall, along with pleasure rides.

KINGSTOWN PAVILION, COUNTY DÚN LAOGHAIRE
BURNED TO A SHELL, 1915

The Kingstown Pavilion and Gardens were built for the cream of Edwardian society in Dublin along with tourists visiting the city. Opened on June 22nd, 1903 the grand structure of wood and glass was intended to replicate aspects of ships, with promenade decks for ladies to stroll across and admire full panoramic view of the mountains and sea. In addition there were elegant wrought iron and glass conservatories to retreat to if it started to rain, or reading rooms – for both gentlemen and ladies – a smoking room, tea rooms and at the heart of the building, a theatre with a grand, 83-feet-wide (25-metre) stage.

William Sheppard, the man responsible for laying out gardens at St. Stephen's Green and the Phoenix Park Zoo, was charged with designing an elegant garden filled with the latest tea roses, imported shrubs, rockeries, fountains and a waterfall. Along with the splendid horticulture, the four-acre site encompassed a band stand, tennis courts and a croquet lawn.

There were two ticket booths on the corner of Marine and Queen's Road and while cabmen with horse-drawn cabs would queue for customers in the early part of the 20th century, they were soon superseded by motorized charabancs.

With the rising popularity of motion pictures the Pavilion soon started running silent movies, that is until the afternoon of November 13th, 1915. A woman who turned up at the venue at 2 p.m. to book tickets for an event found manager Fred Ferne absent and was alarmed by smoke spilling out of the hall into an upstairs corridor.

The 'fireproof paint' proved no match for the inferno and despite the best efforts of the Dublin Corporation and Pembroke Fire Brigades pumping water from the harbour, the Pavilion was reduced to a skeleton by late afternoon. The grand building was gone. In its place a simpler structure, the Pavilion Picture House, was established using the surviving framework and which started showing movies again in 1920.

A new, temporary 850-seat cinema on the site was built in 1935, and despite being made permanent with a solid concrete shell in 1939, suffered the same fate as its predecessor and burned down in November 1940.

Today it is the site of the Pavilion Theatre which opened in 2001 and aims to provide the same variety of entertainment previously offered by the Kingstown Pavilion and Gardens, The Pavilion Picture House and The Pavilion Cinema.

OPPOSITE PAGE The Kingstown Pavilion and Gardens as they looked at the time of opening.

TOP A coloured postcard of the concert hall.

ABOVE Burned out in 1915, the basic structure of the building was salvaged, but the promenades lost.

ABOVE LEFT A 12-seater Albion A3 charabanc of the Kingstown and Bray Motor Services company waits outside the Pavilion Gardens in 1906.

DUBLIN BREAD COMPANY, SACKVILLE STREET, DUBLIN
BURNED 1916

The large and imposing building of the Dublin Bread Company was a landmark on the city's main street, Sackville Street, for the brief period of fifteen years. Built in 1901 it included a restaurant and grill room, as well as a tea room, newsagent's and a hairdressing salon. It offered various musical entertainments on a daily basis. One of its main attractions was the copper-clad, pagoda-like tower which commanded great views of Dublin city and beyond.

The firm had various branches throughout the city, including Dame Street and Stephen's Green. It was usually referred to as the 'D.B.C.' The architect of the six-storey building, George F. Beckett, was only twenty-four years of age when he designed the building. He was later responsible for numerous Methodist churches, technical schools and Carnegie libraries in the city. George Beckett's grandson was the writer, playwright and Nobel laureate Samuel Beckett. The D.B.C. attracted Dubliners from all social classes and its clientele included the nationalist Irish politician Arthur Griffith, who regularly played chess in its smoking rooms. Indeed, it appears that the restaurant was the go-to location for chess players in the city and the Sackville Chess Club was formed there in 1902. The D.B.C. café was also a well-known haunt of young nationalists.

The Dublin Bread Company was George Beckett's first important commission and he utilized a steel frame which was clad in Portland Stone. The first floor was occupied by luncheon rooms, and the smoking rooms were located on the second floor with its balconies and suitably large bow windows. It features in James Joyce's *Ulysses*, where the character Buck Mulligan jokes that D.B.C. stands for 'Damn Bad Cakes'. Local lore also contends that the waitresses liked to joke with British soldiers saying that the D.B.C. on their uniforms meant 'Damnation Before Conscription'.

The strategically important building was taken over by rebels on Easter Monday, 1916, and used to return fire to snipers on the roof of Trinity College. The high tower afforded an excellent observation post. It had been evacuated on Wednesday of the Easter Week. The building was completely destroyed by fire, which had spread from the British bombardment of that block. It is believed that the fire originated in Hoyte's chemist, which contained a lot of turpentine and other combustibles. Its ruins are visible in many of the photographs of the Rising's aftermath. The remains of the building were demolished in July 1916. An insurance claim was lodged by the chairman of the company, John Johnston, for a total £23,932. He was able to give exact costings from the not-too-distant construction of the building. The committee approved the claim.

The chain continued to operate elsewhere in Dublin well into the 20th century. In 1966, the final branch of the D.B.C. at Merrion Row was demolished along with four Georgian houses to make way for an office block.

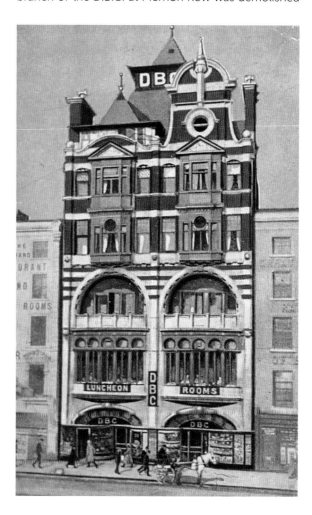

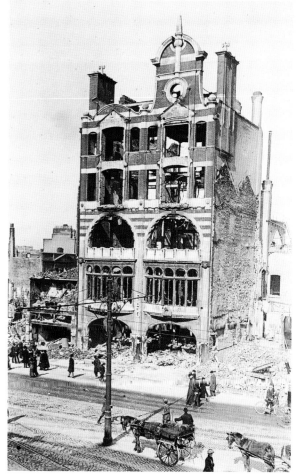

TALLAGHT AERODROME, COUNTY DUBLIN

CLOSED 1919

Tallaght Aerodrome was a World War I Royal Air Force training base in South County Dublin. The site occupied 231 acres and was one of several aerodromes built around Dublin city during this period of rapid expansion for the air force. Others included Baldonnell and Collinstown, both of which are still functioning as airports. Baldonnell went on to become the headquarters of the Irish Air Corps while Collinstown became Dublin International Airport. These locations were chosen as it was felt that locations outside of England would be safer from their German combatants.

Officially known as No. 25 TDS Cookstown, County Dublin, the aerodrome was completed in 1918. The complex consisted of fifty-six buildings, including a photographic hut, a bombing hut, a bomb dropping tower and a machine gun range. It could house seventy-two aircraft in six hangars. Each of the other aerodromes in and around Dublin were built to the same specifications.

Pilots were trained for daytime bombing. The planes which flew from here were designed by the British aircraft firm Avro, which had been founded in Manchester in 1910. Bi-planes designed by Geoffrey de Havilland were also flown from Tallaght.

Many of those who served at Tallaght had previously been based at Biggin Hill in Kent. Members of the Women's Royal Air Force (W.R.A.F.) were also based at Tallaght.

After the conclusion of World War I, the airport was used as a demobilization station for returning troops. The airport's fixtures, fittings and equipment were sold off during several auctions held in 1919. In August of that year the first ever aerial derby in Ireland took place. It involved a race between two planes which took off at the same time from Tallaght Aerodrome and raced to another aerodrome, Gormanstown. The winner was a Captain Urmston.

Overall, the site was deemed to be an unsuitable one for an aerodrome as high winds from nearby mountains caused ongoing problems. In later years part of the site became Urney's chocolate factory, while the rest was devoted to housing. The original factory burnt down in 1924 and the business then

VIEW from HANGAR. TALLAGHT AERODROME

moved to another location in Tallaght. The aerodrome is now the site of the Cookstown Industrial Estate.

OPPOSITE PAGE What is likely to be a final demob photo of trainee pilots and trainers in front of an Avro 504 in 1919. Pilots put on an aerobatic display to mark the closure in August 1919.

ABOVE Tallaght was one of four similar RAF airfields opened near Dublin during World War I, along with Gormanstown, Collinstown and Baldonell. Baldonell was handed over to the Irish Air Service in 1922.

12107. - PATRICK STREET, CORK.

ST. PATRICK'S STREET, CORK
TORCHED 1920

St. Patrick's Street began its ascendancy as the premier shopping street of Cork from the late 18th century. It runs from St. Patrick's Bridge, over the River Lee, in a curve to Daunt Square where it intersects with Grand Parade.

The city of Cork started to expand beyond the city walls during the 1780s and St. Patrick's Street became the main shopping thoroughfare, lined with elegant Victorian buildings, including Grant's Department Store, whose slightly vague motto was, 'The House with the Reputation'. The main branch was on St. Patrick's Street, but there was also a separate furnishings/fancy goods store on Grand Parade.

Cork had achieved international attention with its industrial exhibition of 1852 and from 1898 the Cork Electric Tramway brought shoppers into the centre of the city. The electric trams were ready to transport visitors around the city when Cork hosted its prestigious International Exposition from 1902 to 1903.

However the elegant facades of the buildings along the street were to change irrevocably on the night of December 11th/12th 1920 during the War of Independence. In a shocking reprisal for an earlier IRA ambush of two British army vehicles, the feared Black and Tans (constables recruited from Britain into the Royal Irish Constabulary as reinforcements during the Irish War of Independence) set fire to buildings along St. Patrick's Street, starting with Grant's Department Store. The Georgian City Hall building was also set ablaze and the Munster Arcade destroyed in what was to be known as the Burning of Cork.

St. Patrick's Street was gradually rebuilt in the decade that followed. Grant's replaced their building at No. 51-54 in 1927 and a new City Hall designed by Alfred Jones and Stephen Kelly was completed in 1936.

Ironically, just 22 years after the Burning of Cork, in 1942, Grant's suffered another fire - this time started accidentally - at its 16-18 Grand Parade branch. The fire completely gutted the four-storey building, but it was fully insured for £23,000 and the firm was able to continue trading. Today St Patrick's Street is regularly voted the best shopping street in Ireland.

OPPOSITE PAGE A colourized view of St. Patrick's Street at the turn of the century.

LEFT The Cork City Hall on Albert Quay had started life in 1843 as the city's Corn Exchange. It was replaced by a much larger building in 1936.

BELOW The British government moved swiftly to cover up the actions of their ill-disciplined forces, but a military enquiry laid the blame firmly with the Black and Tans.

THE WEEK-END TERROR IN CORK.

THE SPHERE
DECEMBER 18, 1920

After the Terror—A General View of the Ruins of Patrick Street, Cork

MOYDRUM CASTLE, COUNTY WESTMEATH
BURNED 1921

This ruined castle is located near to Athlone in County Westmeath. It was originally owned by the Handcock family from Devon in England, who were granted lands during the Cromwellian Plantations of Ireland in the 17th century. The Irish architect Richard Morrison redesigned and added to the original house in the Gothic-revival style in the early 19th century. Morrison was well known for his courthouses, hospitals and gaols and for country houses such as Rochestown House in County Tipperary and Mote Park, County Roscommon. It is believed that the now-ruined hunting lodge on nearby Hare Island was also designed by Morrison for the family.

Moydrum was completed in 1814; it had a castellated exterior with both square and round turrets, arched doorcases, and a classical interior. It was situated on the edge of a small lake and surrounded by a wooded demesne.

The house was occupied by the Handcocks until the War of Independence. In July 1921 it was set on fire by members of the Irish Republican Army. The blaze occurred while Lord Castlemaine was in Scotland on a fishing trip; however, his wife, daughter and eight servants were present.

As a member of the House of Lords and someone who regularly had members of the British Army call to the house he was viewed as a legitimate target. The burning was also thought to be in reprisal for the burning of local farmhouses by the much hated Black and Tans. These were constables, mostly from England, recruited into the Royal Irish Constabulary who were considered to be less well trained and more ruthless than the existing force. The family and servants were given time to leave the house and to gather a few items; however, most of their possessions were lost and the blaze completely destroyed the castle. Several of the servants were charged with looting items from the house, including a fur coat. Lord Castlemaine received compensation from the state for the destruction of his property and much of the estate was sold to the Land Commission in the 1920s. Following the fire the family resided permanently in England.

In 1984, the ruined castle featured on the cover of U2's fourth album, *The Unforgettable Fire*. While the title is a reference to the atomic bombing of the Japanese city of Hiroshima in 1945, it also aptly fitted the castle's fate. The photograph was taken by Anton Corbijn; however, its publication resulted in the band having to compensate a photographer named Simon Marsden who claimed that it was identical to the photograph on the front of his 1980 publication on the ruined houses of Ireland. Both photographers used an infrared filter which accentuated the ivy and foliage that had grown on the ruin. Many U2 fans from around the world come to see the ruins, which are now in private hands. A ruined church which was once used by the family is also on the grounds.

OPPOSITE PAGE Located in the Irish midlands, the Gothic-revival castle was designed by Richard Morrison.

LEFT The castle is best known as the cover image of U2's 1984 album *The Unforgettable Fire*. U2 recorded some of the album at Slane Castle in County Meath.

PUBLIC RECORD OFFICE / FOUR COURTS, DUBLIN

DESTROYED / GUTTED 1922

The Public Record Office of Ireland was located in a purpose-built, six-storey archive building attached to the rear of the Four Courts. The impressive neoclassical building housed the four courts of Chancery, King's Bench, Exchequer and Common Pleas. It was Ireland's main court building and was constructed between 1786 and 1796. The Public Record Office was established in 1867 and it held the records of seven centuries of Irish history, including individual census returns containing the demographic record for pre-Famine Ireland. It also housed medieval manuscripts and records of births, deaths and wills. Known as the Record Treasury the building had 30-foot-high (9-metre) windows, ornamental ironwork and an expansive glass ceiling. It contained 100,000 square feet of shelving. The architect for the Record Treasury was James H. Owen. Owen had previously worked on large government projects such as the Criminal Lunatic Asylum in Dundrum.

Herbert Wood, Assistant Deputy Keeper of the Office, published a complete account of the office's holdings in 1919. London-born Wood had joined the staff in 1884. The completion of the 300-page *Guide to the Records Deposited in the Public Record Office of Ireland* represented a phenomenal undertaking. The task was delayed by cutbacks and staff shortages during World War I. Less than three years later disaster struck when, on the 30th of June 1922, the office and the majority of the records it held were destroyed during the Civil War.

The Civil War had broken out in 1921 between those who did or did not accept the terms of the treaty with Britain which heralded the partitioning of Ireland. The Four Courts was occupied by the Anti-Treaty Irregulars in April 1922. The new Free State Army attacked the Four Courts and, after a two-day bombardment, fire destroyed the building when mines stored in the basement exploded. The central dome collapsed, and it was reported that fragments of charred archives and manuscripts wafted along the quays. Staff gathered what they could, and partially burnt 1821 census returns do survive, albeit only for certain counties. Wood resigned from the post of Deputy Keeper in March 1923 citing that is was as a consequence of the destruction of the Public Record Office.

The rebuilding of the Four Courts took ten years, and when it was reopened in 1932 it lacked much of its interior details. The Public Record Office had reopened in 1928 on a much-reduced scale and without the purpose-built facilities of its previous incarnation. Following the establishment of the National Archives of Ireland in 1988, the records from the Four Courts were merged with the State Paper Office files held at the Record Tower in Dublin Castle. Both collections were moved to the National Archives building in Bishop Street in 1991.

In 2018, a collaborative project called Beyond 2022 was established to recreate the building and contents of the office. Taking Wood's catalogue as its basis it hopes to identify substitute records held in Ireland and elsewhere and to open and conserve some of the documents which were collected by the P.R.O.I. staff and wrapped in brown paper parcels nearly one hundred years ago.

OPPOSITE PAGE The beautiful Four Courts building with the Public Record Office behind and adjoining.

BELOW The Four Courts rotunda on fire in April 1922. The Public Record Office and priceless documents were lost in the fire. There has been an immense effort to obtain copies of duplicate documents held in other archives to redress some of the loss.

FOUR COURTS. DUBLIN. 1655. W L.

MITCHELSTOWN CASTLE, COUNTY CORK
TORCHED 1922

'Mitchelstown Castle, the splendid seat of the Earl of Kingston, is a noble and sumptuous structure of hewn stone, in the castellated style, erected after a design by Mr. Pain, of Cork, at an expense of more than £100,000.'

So wrote Samuel Lewis in his 1837 *Topographical Dictionary of Ireland*. There had been a castle on the site since the fifteenth century. Through marriage it had passed to the Barons and Earls of Kingston. Most of the old Mitchelstown Castle was demolished in the 1770s and a remainder of the old building incorporated into a modern Palladian-style mansion. It was during this time that proto-feminist, the 27-year-old Mary Wollstonecraft travelled to Ireland to take up a new post as governess to the three daughters of Lord and Lady Kingsborough at Mitchelstown. In a storyline straight from a Jane Austen novel, one of the girls later eloped with Henry Fitzgerald who was shot and killed by her enraged father, the 2nd Earl.

The freespending George Kingsborough, 3rd Earl of Kingston, had new plans for the building. In 1823, after his succession to the title, he demolished the Palladian house and replaced it with a massive neo-Gothic house with a 100-foot (30-metre) gallery, sixty principal bedrooms, three libraries, and a dining room capable of seating a hundred guests.

Despite the enormous price tag it reinforced a trend for the admiring Irish nobility and Strancally Castle (County Waterford) and Dromoland Castle continued the trend, though neither were as extensive as Mitchelstown.

The excessive spending on the house was ill-timed; the estate suffered a series of financial setbacks in the 19th century and after the Great Famine of the 1840s was forced to sell 70,000 of its 100,000 acres. Family disputes and the Land War of the 1880s put strain on the family finances as well as their relationship with the local population, many of whom were evicted from the estate's properties.

In June 1922 the owners of Mitchelstown Castle experienced forcible eviction themselves when it was occupied by the Irish Republican Army, and in August of that year the contents were looted and the house set on fire. It became notorious as the largest house in Ireland destroyed either during the War of Independence (1919-1921) or the Civil War (1922-1923). Afterwards, the owner William Downes Webber, sought compensation from the Irish Free State to rebuild the property, a claim pursued after his death in 1924 by Colonel W. A. King-Harman.

In 1926 an Irish High Court judge ruled that the destruction of Mitchelstown Castle had been an act of wanton destruction with no military purpose, however the money awarded in the judgement was a fraction of what it would have cost to rebuild the castle. King-Harman decided to spend his compensation on new properties in Dublin instead, while the stones of Mitchelstown Castle were eventually sold to the monks of Mount Melleray Abbey in County Waterford – a much higher calling.

OPPOSITE PAGE Moydrum Castle had already been built when George Kingsborough commissioned his extravagant neo-Gothic pile. The ice house belonging to the original 1780 Palladian mansion still remains, to the west of the site, now on the other side of the Mitchelstown bypass.

The Boyne Obelisk, also known as King Billy's Obelisk, was a structure near Oldbridge, County Louth that was erected to commemorate William III's victory over King James II at the Battle of the Boyne. The foundation stone was laid in April 1736 by Lionel Sackville, the Duke of Dorset, who was Lord Lieutenant of Ireland at the time.

The obelisk, made from granite, carried an inscription which read: 'This monument was erected by the grateful contributions of several protestants of Great Britain and Ireland', and commemorated the crossing of the river by the forces of William III on the 1st of July 1690, prior to his defeat of the army of James II. The battle is historic for many reasons, but it was the last time that two crowned kings of England, Scotland and Ireland faced each other on the battlefield. After William's victory, Protestantism gained ascendancy in Ireland and James II was forced into exile.

Located on the edge of the River Boyne, near Drogheda, the monument was over 164 feet (50 metres) high and purported to be set on the actual location where the Duke of Schomberg, a member of William's army, was killed.

The obelisk has been the subject of several works of art, including prints and engravings made after Paul Sandby's *Obelisk in Memory of the Battle of the Boyne*. Sandby was an English landscape painter who was also a founding member of the Royal Academy. In the 1870s, the American printmakers Currier and Ives produced a coloured lithographic view of the obelisk and river entitled *The Boyne Water*. The Irish artist Andrew Nicholl also captured the obelisk in his watercolour *The Boyne Obelisk, with Cattle Watering*, after which steel engravings were made by Thomas Jeavons.

Perhaps the most intriguing artistic depiction is Thomas Mitchell's *A View of the River Boyne with Gentlemen and Horses by a Statue to William III in the Foreground, the Boyne Obelisk Beyond* (1757). While accurate with regard to the placing and inclusion of the obelisk, the inclusion of the statue is puzzling as none was known to exist on this site. In fact, the statue appears to be very similar to the equestrian one by Grinling Gibbons erected at College Green and discussed elsewhere in this book. The painting, which is in the collection of the National Museums of Northern Ireland, shows an idealized landscape bathed in a hazy light and was most likely painted during Mitchell's visit to Ireland in 1757. Popular prints showing the obelisk were still in circulation over a hundred years after its erection and this provides an indicator of the site's continued significance to the unionist communities.

The location has been the scene of political turmoil: a man called Patrick Briscoe, a herder on a nearby estate, was shot and killed at the obelisk, as he returned from a volunteer parade. In May 1923, during the Civil War, the monument was blown up using dynamite taken from a nearby barracks. The stump remains in situ and sections of the monument were taken to Belfast; they are now on display there at the Museum of Orange Heritage.

OPPOSITE PAGE When it was completed in 1736, the Boyne Obelisk was the tallest man-made structure in Ireland.

LEFT The inscription on the south side of the monument read: 'Marshal the Duke of Schomberg in passing this river died bravely fighting.' A nearby house that King William stayed in at the time of the battle is known as 'Schomberg Cottage'.

TRANSATLANTIC CABLE STATIONS, COUNTY KERRY

BALLINSKELLIGS CLOSED 1923

For a period in the late 19th and early 20th centuries a remote stretch of the Kerry coast in West Ireland was a telecommunications hotspot. Laying of cables from this region began as early as the 1850s and the first transatlantic telegraph was sent by Queen Victoria to the President of the United States, James Buchanan, via a cable station on Valentia Island in August 1858.

A commercial cable company set up in Kerry in 1866 and the Valentia station became the first permanent link between Europe and America. It linked Heart's Content, Newfoundland to Valentia Island. The laying of these cables across the Atlantic Ocean from Kerry to Newfoundland was a spectacular engineering feat. The German company Siemens laid cables with their specially designed ship the *Faraday*, which was active laying thousands of miles of cables from 1874 into the 20th century. There were several cable stations facilitating transatlantic communication, and other locations included Waterville and Ballinskelligs. The station at Ballinskelligs was established in 1874. These cable stations were run by several private companies, including the Anglo-American Telegraph Company at Valentia and the British-owned Direct United States Telegraph Company at Ballinskelligs. On the opposite side of the Atlantic, operations were largely run by the Western Union Telegraph Company.

The architect of the station at Waterville was James Franklin Fuller whose other works included churches, hospitals and several Church of Ireland schools. Many of those employed in the cable stations came from outside Ireland and these highly skilled and well-paid workers provided a valuable cash injection into the area. A vibrant social life sprung up with golf, cricket matches and dances taking place.

The 1901 and 1911 censuses show that many of the cable operators were English-born single men, although some local people were also employed. Workers were listed as cable operators, telegraph mechanics and telegram engineers, including English-born Harold James Cross, who described himself as an 'Electricman on a Radio Telegraph Station'.

By the time of the Easter Rising in 1916, it was estimated that the majority of the employees at the cable stations in Valentia and Ballinskelligs were Irish-born, while half of the staff in Valentia were native born. During World War I, there was increased government communication across the Atlantic, and censors were deployed to the cable stations. The communications issued from the station with regard to the Easter Rising in 1916 were subject to censorship; however, some of the local employees were favourably disposed towards the Rising and the local Ring brothers sent communications which were counter to company rules. They were arrested under the 1914 Defence of the Realm Act and the activities of the stations were placed under further scrutiny. During the disturbances of the Civil War the service was diverted to Penzance in Cornwall.

The Ballinskelligs cable station closed in 1923 and the buildings became government property, used as a summer college for Irish language students. They later fell into disrepair and most have now been demolished.

The nearby Waterville and Valentia stations remained open until the 1960s. Some of the cable station buildings in Waterville have been refurbished and now act as holiday homes.

OPPOSITE PAGE The Ballinskelligs Station pictured in the late 19th century.

FAR LEFT It is thought that the striped poles visible in this photograph were used to warn fishing vessels of the underwater cables.

LEFT Such was the interest in a transatlantic telegraph that polkas, quicksteps, marches and waltzes were composed in its honour.

ABLE STATION. BALLINSKELLEGS. Co. KERRY. 3066 W.L

BALLYBUNION MONORAILWAY, COUNTY KERRY
HIT THE BUFFERS 1924

Inspired by watching camels carrying heavy loads in panniers strapped either side of their backs, French engineer Charles Lartigue developed his own unique monorail system. Strictly speaking it wasn't a monorail as it required a stabilising rail on either side, but it was clearly different to any conventional railway in Ireland.

The Listowel to Ballybunion line in North Kerry linked the two towns on an 8.9-mile (14.4-kilometre) route and was opened in February 1888. The advantage of a Lartigue Railway was that it was easy and cheaper to build than a conventional rail track, but there were considerable operating drawbacks. With a central divide in carriages, passengers couldn't move across from side to side. To get to the other side of the train there was a footbridge carriage, with steps at the back. In the freight cars, loads had to be balanced, and so a cow on one side had to be balanced by milk churns on the other.

Whereas conventional railways had level crossings, the raised nature of the Lartigue system meant that small drawbridges had to be installed to carry roads over the monorail (pictured). Where this wasn't possible, a turntable or swing bridge principle was used to disengage a section of rail, swing it round so that vehicles or animals could pass, before the rail was swung back into place. Naturally, these were linked to signals, so that an approaching train would be warned of either in progress.

The Ballybunion line ran three specially built locomotives. Because of the even weight distribution needed, each had two boilers and two fireboxes, one stoked by the fireman, the other by the driver.

Although the system was not widely adapted in Europe, the line ran until the Civil War in 1922 during which some of the track and rolling stock was damaged. In the aftermath, when rail lines were amalgamated under the Great Southern Railways in the Irish Free State, the failure to include Ballybunion-Listowel proved its death knell and it closed in October 1924.

In 2003, the Lartigue Monorailway Restoration Committee managed to re-open a kilometre-long section of the line on part of its former trackbed to give a taste of travel in the steam age. Sadly, none of

the old 0-3-0 locomotives built by the Hunslet Engine Company have survived and today demonstration runs are pulled by a diesel engine constructed to look like one of the originals. But at least they don't have to stoke two fireboxes.

OPPOSITE PAGE TOP Each train needed at least one footbridge carriage to allow passengers to cross from one side to the other. This one had two.

OPPOSITE PAGE BOTTOM LEFT The 'saddlebag' nature of the carriages made it impossible to pass from side to side in the compartment.

OPPOSITE PAGE BOTTOM RIGHT With a track height of over a metre, a unique switching system had to be devised to route the trains.

ABOVE Level crossings on the monorailway were an elaborate drawbridge construction.

RIGHT A reconstructed diesel Lartigue engine still runs on a short section of track.

KING WILLIAM STATUE, DUBLIN

Royal statues were often the victims of politically motivated attacks and none more so than the College Green statue of King William III, otherwise known as William of Orange. His victory over the Catholic King James at the Battle of the Boyne in 1690 consolidated the power of the Protestant throne.

Grinling Gibbons was commissioned to design an equestrian statue of the king and a contract was signed on the 9th of April, 1700. Made of lead, the equestrian statue was unveiled on the 1st of July 1701, on the eleventh anniversary of the Battle of the Boyne. Gibbons was also commissioned by King William III to create carvings, some of which adorn Kensington Palace. He was employed by Christopher Wren to work on St. Paul's Cathedral in London and later appointed as master carver to George I.

The statue is the focus point of Francis Wheatley's gigantic historical painting *The Dublin Volunteers on College Green, 4th November, 1779*. The volunteers were a militia formed from the Protestant ascendancy initially to defend against possible French invasion; however, they also lobbied for legislative independence from Britain. Wheatley pictured them marching to King William's statue and demonstrating for free trade between Ireland and England.

For those in favour of the Act of Union of 1801 (which saw the Irish parliament removed to London and Ireland joined to Britain), William of Orange also symbolized their world view and loyalties. The statue became a focus for unionists throughout the 19th and early 20th centuries and thus a target for those seeking independence and a republic.

As early as 1710, drunken students from nearby Trinity College were charged with damaging the statue. His sword and truncheon were repeatedly broken off, and in 1715 the city decided to build a watch house beside the statue and post a couple of sentinels there. In 1798 his sword was again removed and there was an attempt to saw off his head. In 1805, supporters of Catholic Emancipation covered the horse with a mixture of tar and grease, while in 1837 the figure was blown completely off the horse. Railings were also put around it to protect it from protesters.

The statue features in James Joyce's short story *The Dead*, where the main character, Gabriel's grandfather, was noted as riding his horse around the statue repeatedly, signifying Ireland's paralysis and failure to advance.

The statue was eventually removed in 1929 following an explosion in the early hours of Armistice Day. Fragments of the plinth remain, and a marble plaque depicting military motifs was exhibited along with William III's lead head at a Tate Britain exhibition entitled *Art Under Attack: Histories of British Iconoclasm* in 2013.

William of Orange's statue at College Green was not the only royal statue to be attacked in Dublin. Another royal equestrian statue, this one depicting George II on horseback, was also bombed on Armistice Day, although the damage was minimal. However, another bomb in 1937 caused more severe damage and toppled that statue from its pedestal.

IRISH INTERNATIONAL GRAND PRIX, PHOENIX PARK

CLOSED 1931

This short-lived event ran between 1929 and 1931 in the Phoenix Park on the north side of the capital city. Motor racing had taken place in the park since 1903. The 4.25-mile (6.8-kilometre) circuit followed a route along the main avenue and along the edges of the vast green space. The event actually consisted of two different races: one for vehicles up to 1500cc and the other for more powerful engines. The two cups awarded were the Saorstát Cup and the Éireann Cup. It was organized by the Royal Irish Automobile Club (R.I.A.C.), which had their headquarters on Dawson Street, Dublin. Established in 1901, it is one of the oldest automobile clubs in the world.

One of the obstacles that the organizers had to overcome was the removal of the Phoenix Column, which was located in the centre of Chesterfield Avenue, the main thoroughfare that runs through the park. The Portland stone monument, which dated from 1747, was removed and installed elsewhere in the park. It was only reinstated on the avenue in the 1990s.

The Grand Prix was considered to be the first international sporting event organized by the independent Irish Free State, and as such the Fine Gael party government were keen to demonstrate their competency and organizational skills. They assisted with the building of the 250-yard-long (228-metre) grandstands which spanned Chesterfield Avenue and provided a grant for the running of the event.

The first Grand Prix took place on the 12th and 13th of July 1929 and covered a 300-mile (483-kilometre) distance. The race commenced with an exciting standing, or Le Mans-style start where cars were stationery when the race began (but with engines running) and drivers had to run across the track to their cars. Both races were won by a Russian driver called Boris Ivanowski in an Alfa Romeo. He beat England's Glen Kidston who drove a Bentley. Government ministers and their wives occupied seats in the grandstand and an estimated 100,000 spectators turned up for the first event, which received high praise from the international and racing press.

The following year, the event was somewhat hampered by bad weather. A railway strike meant that the public did not attend in as high numbers as before. A change of government in 1931 put an end to state support for the race which some considered to be a rich man's sport. Politicians objected that citizens had to pay to enter a public park. They also noted that there were no Irish drivers and many members of the new Fianna Fáil government saw it as adding little or no advantage to the country.

Neither the wooden pit buildings nor the viewing stands were permanent and the Grand Prix left no lasting mark on the Phoenix Park.

OPPOSITE PAGE The start of the Saorstát Cup race in 1930.

BELOW Motor racing continued in Phoenix Park, but without a headline international grand prix. This race from 1936.

EUCHARISTIC CONGRESS HIGH ALTAR, DUBLIN
DISMANTLED 1932

The 31st International Eucharistic Congress was a five-day-long celebration of the Roman Catholic sacrament of the Eucharist and took place in Dublin in June 1932. Over one million people attended and it attracted Irish and international pilgrims, clergy and bishops from all over the world. It was opened to much fanfare with an aerial fly-over marking the arrival of the papal legate (the personal representative of the pope in foreign nations) Cardinal Lorenzo Lauri. The largest event was an open-air Mass in Phoenix Park. Pilgrims were encouraged to think of the entire city as a sacred space and the streets were adorned with bunting and altars. Six ocean liners were moored in Dublin Bay and they acted as floating hotels accommodating pilgrims.

The Irish government saw this as an opportunity to showcase the fledgling state on an international platform, revealing their ability to organize a peaceful mass event. The Congress required the construction of several temporary buildings throughout the city and these revealed a mix of both modernity and tradition in their design and conception. The new state sought to project a new identity for Ireland which heightened the aspects of its past and differentiated it from its former rulers, and the Catholic nature of this event perfectly fitted the bill.

Technology was employed in the form of an advanced loudspeaker system which relayed the Mass throughout the city. A construction of a new radio transmission station in Athlone was accelerated in order to allow the transmission of the services across the country and to the wider world. In contrast, the designers also relied upon symbolism derived from early Christian Ireland; for example, the Round Tower which was erected at College Green in the city centre. The High Altar in Phoenix Park referenced the Baroque architecture of the Vatican. The Catholic Church was a master of propaganda and ensured that the event was publicized in dramatic photographs. Photography was incorporated into the design of temporary buildings such as the High Altar, which included portholes in the main colonnades to facilitate press photographers and ensure that the crowd in its totality could be captured. The Irish Air Corps were deployed to photograph the

vast crowds and the shots were widely published along with panoramic images revealing the scale of the crowds. The positioning of the Round Tower was telling as it was located on the site of a statue of King William III of Orange, which was emblematic of the loyalist and pre-independence regime.

The organizers also wished to ensure that the route taken by the papal legate showed the country in a good light and several triumphal arches were constructed along the route into the city. Some were quite simple and many were decorated with the papal and Eucharistic insignia. Decorations were organized along parish lines and even the poorest of tenement houses, which were not on the official routes, put up their own arches, altars and bunting.

TOP The High Altar in Phoenix Park.

ABOVE Where a year previously grand prix cars had raced at 100 mph plus, crowds flocked to Ireland's most prestigious religious event.

OPPOSITE PAGE The procession route for the papal legate passed over O'Connell Bridge.

CLADDAGH. GALWAY. 6185 W.L.

THE CLADDAGH, GALWAY CITY
DEMOLISHED 1934

The Claddagh was a fishing village lying just outside Galway's city walls at the point where the Corrib flows into Galway Bay. The word 'claddagh' means 'shore' in the Irish language. The village had retained a separate identity, with its residents speaking Irish and wearing traditional clothing longer than those who were resident inside the city walls.

The Claddagh fishermen used a traditional fishing boat called a Galway hooker which was unique to Galway Bay and the Connemara coast. Its distinctive red-brown sails contrasted with the pitch black boat. In 1836, there were 105 of these open sailboats based at the Claddagh. They sold their fish at the market on the opposite side of the river, near to the Spanish Arch.

The Piscatorial School at the Claddagh was set up in 1846 (during the Famine) by the Dominican religious order to teach local children basic reading and writing skills as well as practical skills such a making fish nets for boys and sewing and spinning for girls. The three-storey building could accommodate three hundred children. It was topped with a statue of a fisherman made from red chalk. It subsequently operated as a primary school. The school was sold despite calls from local community groups for it to be bought by the city council.

The village lent its name to the Claddagh ring. Originating in the 17th century, it shows two hands clasped around a crowned heart. A version of the ring has been produced in Galway since at least 1700; however, it was not called Claddagh until the 1730s. Dillon's jewellers were credited with the revival of the rings and they are still made and sold in the city.

Colour photos of the Claddagh taken in 1913 using the autochrome process are some of the earliest colour photographs taken in Ireland. They were produced as part of the *Archives of the Planet* project financed by the French banker Albert Kahn, which sought to create a worldwide inventory of traditional communities. The photographs were taken by two Frenchwomen, Marguerite Mespoulet and Madeleine Mignon-Alba and show women wearing the distinctive Galway cloaks amid the stone cottages of the Claddagh.

The original village of thatched cottages was a popular tourist attraction and a stop-off point for

TOP Children ask for pennies from a tourist in the early 1930s.

ABOVE One of the famous Musée Albert Kahn photos of 1913.

OPPOSITE PAGE It may have looked like a picture postcard Irish village with traditional thatched cottages, but there was real poverty in Claddagh.

those leaving the city en route to the beauty spots of Connemara. Following a deadly outbreak of tuberculosis in 1927 it was decided that the unsanitary conditions at the Claddagh should be addressed through the demolition of the existing thatched houses. A 1927 newspaper article announced that a hundred three-bedroomed houses were to be built in their place. Demolition and rebuilding took place in the 1930s; however, many in the village complained about a lack of consultation with the existing community. Some argued that existing houses should have been upgraded rather than razed. Concerns were also brought up as to the fishermen's ability to pay the new council rents, the dispersal of the population, and the fairness of the compensation offered to those whose homes were destroyed. Even though the traditional cottages were replaced by council houses the area retains a strong community to this day; nonetheless the failure to retain the unique village represents a loss for the city of Galway.

OPPOSITE PAGE Men of the Claddagh had the exclusive rights to fish in Galway Bay. Any outsider risked having his nets cut and his boat damaged. There was an annual vote for an elected king among the fishermen, and the king governed the fleet; leading them out to sea and resolving disputes.

ABOVE Claddagh's downfall was the unsanitary conditions of its housing. A deadly outbreak of Tuberculosis hit the community hard in 1927.

RIGHT A traditional street vendor. A fishing community had been recorded in Claddagh since the fifth century.

DUNSCOMBE FOUNTAIN, CORK CITY
REMOVED 1935

This temperance fountain was located at the foot of Shandon Street near to the North Gate bridge in the centre of Cork city. It was gifted by the well-established Dunscombe family, in April 1883, in memory of Reverend Nicholas Colthurst Dunscombe, a leader of the temperance movement. Several members of this merchant family, which had links to the city going back to the 17th century, had become lord mayors of Cork. Their impressive home was located on the banks of the River Lee overlooking the city. Another member of the family was Richard Dunscombe Parker who was best known for his paintings of native Irish birds.

In the 19th century, sanitation was poor in many cities and drinking water was often linked to outbreaks of deadly diseases such as cholera. As a result of this, many city dwellers did not trust the water supplies and resorted to drinking beer, as fermented beverages were less likely to bring disease. Of course this did not win favour with the growing temperance movement and they sought to provide a free, clean and safe alternative to alcoholic beverages by providing drinking fountains.

Associations were set up in Britain and Ireland in order to raise funds for the erection and maintenance of these fountains. It is not surprising that such a fountain was erected in Cork as the city had a long tradition of temperance campaigns directed towards both the Protestant and Catholic communities. The initial anti-drink movement of the 1820s and 1830s was mainly run by Protestants; however, a Cork-based Catholic priest, Father Theobald Mathew, initiated a highly successful mass temperance movement in the 1840s when over three million people signed up to his total abstinence pledge.

The Dunscombe fountain was built by George Smith & Company's Sun Foundry in Glasgow. A central column with an engraved dedication supported an inverted umbrella-style canopy with highly decorated acanthus scrollwork. A supply of cups attached to chains was also part of the design. At one stage it had glass globes lit by gas, but these were gone by the 1930s.

The fountain appears to have offered the people of Cork a natural gathering point. Holly and Ivy were sold at Christmas-time and street vendors also sold clothes at its base. Women pictured in the photos are seen wearing traditional shawls. Known as 'shawlies' these working-class women traded on the city's streets and later in the 20th century often came into conflict with authorities who tried to regulate street trading. The vibrant street life pictured in these images shows a busy streetscape with Jones' pawnbrokers and Connolly paint sellers visible in the background. The photographs were taken by an unnamed member of the Cork Camera Club around 1930.

The committee that was established to administer the fountain was active between 1883 and the fountain's removal in 1935. Its current whereabouts are unknown. It is quite hard to believe that something so large and unwieldy could disappear without a trace and that no record was kept of the monument's disposal.

OPPOSITE PAGE AND ABOVE The iron fountain was topped with a gas light. In 2017 local councillor Kenneth O'Flynn asked the council what had happened to it – a question they could not answer.

ACHILL SOUND STATION, COUNTY MAYO

CLOSED 1937

A 27-mile (43-kilometre) branch line connected the remote island of Achill off the coast of Mayo to the towns of Westport and Newport. Run by the Midland Great Western Railway company, the Achill Sound station was on the mainland, a short boat trip across from Achill Island. The branch line started service in 1895 as an extension of the Dublin to Westport line and did much to open up Achill Island to tourists. The line was considered to be one of the so-called Balfour lines. This relates to the legislation introduced by an earlier Lord Lieutenant of Ireland, Arthur J. Balfour, who passed an act which granted monies towards the construction of railways in disadvantaged areas on the West coast of the country. The route along the line was one of the most scenic in Ireland and passed through Mulranny and Newport and the Corraun Peninsula before arriving at Achill Sound.

The opening and closing of the line coincided with two tragedies which befell Achill's inhabitants. Both related to emigration. On the 14th of June 1894, thirty-two islanders drowned when a hooker (a native type of sail boat) sank in Clew Bay. The occupants were on their way to Scotland via Westport to engage in potato picking or 'tattie-hooking'. A special train was brought into operation to transport the bodies home. Many are buried in Kildownet Cemetery; the gravestone there reveals that most were young women and many families had multiple bereavements. However, despite the tragedy, the tradition of seasonal migration to Scotland continued.

In September 1937, ten migrant workers from the island were burnt to death in a bothy (a small hut used to house farm labourers) at Kirkintilloch, Scotland. The bodies of the young men were returned via the same train line. Two weeks later the Achill Island railway line closed. It is believed locally that these deaths were foretold in the 17th century by Brian Rua Ó Ceabháin, who prophesied that a carriage on iron wheels would bring home the dead to Achill on its first and last journey.

The first official train ran in 1895 and individual towns prospered with the introduction of the line. Railway companies introduced combined rail and hotel tickets and stops along the route boomed.

Many railway companies also built and ran hotels; for example, the Mulranny Park Hotel along the Achill line was built by the Midland Great Western company in 1897. This company amalgamated with the Great Southern Railway in 1924. The passenger line was closed down in 1937 and a large section of steel tracks were taken up and sold to Germany.

The trackbed of the branch line now forms a Greenway, which allows cycling from Westport to Achill Island. It is the longest off-road cycling and walking trail in Ireland. Its reopening involved lengthy discussions with landlords, as much of the property along the route had returned to private ownership. The Achill Sound train station has been converted into a hostel to meet the needs of those on the trail.

OPPOSITE PAGE The opening of the branch line in 1894 contributed to local commerce and was a boon to tourists keen to visit the site of Grace O'Malley's Castle on Achill Island. The island was linked to the mainland by bridge in 1887.

BELOW The view from the station to Achill Sound.

ACHILL SOUND. 5083. W.L.

RAILWAY STATION ACHILL 5082 W L

VALLEYS FLOODED BY 1940

In the early decades of the independent Irish state, the government initiated several large-scale hydroelectric projects which were aimed at attaining self-sufficiency in power generation. These included the Shannon hydroelectric scheme, which harnessed the power of the country's largest river. It involved damming the River Shannon, and the spectacular Ardnacrusha generating plant was opened in 1929.

The second scheme was planned for the east of the country. Built between 1937 and 1947, the project involved the damming of the River Liffey and flooding several townlands. A dam was proposed at Poulaphouca (meaning 'Pool of the Pooka', where 'Pooka' means a male demon or ghost). Some 5,600 acres (2,250 hectares) of land were to be flooded. Compulsory purchase orders were issued on farms and seventy-six houses. These were demolished and bridges at Humphreystown, Baltyboys and Burgage were blown up. A graveyard at Burgage was moved to the north, to higher ground on the outskirts of Blessington. A high cross dating from the 12th century, known as St. Mark's Cross or St. Baoithin's Cross was moved when its original site was destined to be submerged by the works.

The Poulaphouca Falls were also affected by the building of the associated hydroelectric scheme which reduced the flow of water over the Falls. This had been a tourist attraction and beauty spot from as early as the 18th century. It was a popular subject for engravings, prints and postcards. An extension of the Dublin and Blessington Steam Tramway terminated at Poulaphouca and it was popular with day-trippers. It

OPPOSITE PAGE The Poulaphouca (alternatively Pollaphuca or Poulaphuca) Falls were a tourist attraction, spanned by a Gothic-revival bridge. The bridge survives just below the dam, but the hydroelectric installation has restricted the flow of water.

BELOW Some of the housing stock that was swallowed up by the reservoir. In all, seventy-six houses from Blessington, Ballyknockan and Ballinahown were submerged along with 5,600 acres of farmland.

opened in 1895 and closed in 1932.

Those who owned farms in the area were compensated; however, no payments were made to the landless and those who lost their occupations. Some of the families were moved out of the region to County Kildare. Communities were uprooted and many felt that the compensation offered was insufficient.

In 1938/39 the region was surveyed by Liam Price, Caoimhín Ó Danachair and the Folklore Department at University College Dublin. This survey studied vernacular housing types and the farming practices and customs that existed in the valley before it was flooded in 1940.

The reservoir still supplies electricity for the national grid and water for the Dublin area. The man-made Blessington Lakes are now a Special Area of Conservation and a site for birdwatching. During the hot summer of 2018 water levels in the reservoir dropped, revealing the ruins of farmhouses and the abandoned farm machinery which had not been seen since they were submerged many decades previously. Photographs showed the remnants of a tree-lined road and carts and wagons, which had been left by the farmers nearly ninety years before.

OPPOSITE PAGE Several old bridges across the Liffey were lost including this ancient bridge at Humphreystown, along with Old Burgage Bridge and Blessington Bridge

BELOW Work on damming the Liffey commences at Poulaphouca with concrete supplied by the Francois Cementation Company.

BOTTOM A modern-day view looking down on the Blessington Lakes formed by damming the Liffey. In times of drought, eerie visions of times past emerge from the reservoir – rusty farm machinery, old corn stands and crumbled farmsteads.

DOUBLE-DECKER TRAMS, DUBLIN

CEASED TO OPERATE 1940s

The Dublin tram service began in 1872 with a route between College Green and the suburb of Rathgar. Originally, the double-decker carriages were pulled by two horses, with the passengers on the upper deck exposed to the elements.

The service was run by a variety of small private companies at first; however, William Martin Murphy's Dublin United Tramways Company (D.U.T.C.) eventually gained a near monopoly. From the 1890s onwards, the double-decker trams were electrified. This process took several years and the last horse-drawn tram ran in 1901. By the end of the 19th century, the system had expanded significantly, with a comprehensive network of 66 miles (106 kilometres) of electric tramlines.

In addition to radial routes originating in the city centre, there were several routes linking suburbs together; for example the Donnybrook to Phoenix Park route and the Rathfarnham to Drumcondra route, which also took in Harold's Cross. Nelson's Pillar on Sackville (later O'Connell) Street was a hub for the transport network as the trams had their main terminus located there.

The D.U.T.C. trams were built in Ireland at the Spa Road works in Inchicore, Dublin. Examples of these Dublin-built carriages can be found in the National Transport Museum in Howth. Competition from buses finally saw a decline in tram usership and the last trams ran in the 1940s.

Fragments of the infrastructure remain in place today in the guise of rails and buildings bearing the D.U.T.C. name and logo. A limited, though very successful, light rail tramway system known as the LUAS (the word in Irish means speed) was reintroduced to Dublin in 2004. By 2006, over fifty million journeys had been taken on the system. The two-line tramway was augmented in 2017; however, its reach is nowhere near that of the tram network of the late 19th and early 20th centuries.

OPPOSITE PAGE The Dalkey tram passes famous Dublin merchant Alex Findlater's store at 84 and 85 Lower George Street in Dún Laoghaire.

BELOW LEFT Trams swarm across the O'Connell Bridge in the 1930s.

BELOW Double-decker horse-drawn trams took over from the original single-deckers.

BOTTOM The extension of the tram system was of tremendous benefit to developers enlarging the Dublin suburbs.

QUEEN VICTORIA MEMORIAL. DUBLIN. 9648. W.L.

QUEEN VICTORIA STATUE, LEINSTER LAWN, DUBLIN

REMOVED 1948

On the 17th of February 1908, a rather unflattering bronze statue of the late Queen Victoria was unveiled on Leinster Lawn, Dublin. The sculptor John Hughes was the instructor of modelling at the nearby Metropolitan School of Art (later National College of Art and Design). Made of bronze and cast in Paris, the statue was 4.6 metres (15 feet) high and stood on a limestone plinth surrounded by marble cherubs. Acting as both a war memorial and a tribute to the Queen, the base was adorned with several figures depicting Ireland or Hibernia at War and Peace. War was represented by a dying Irish soldier embodying the sacrifice of Irishmen in the Boer War. The figure of Erin (representing Ireland) stands behind him clutching a wreath.

The statue was never particularly popular with Dubliners; however, with Ireland's independence from British rule in 1922, it became an even more contentious presence. Especially as Leinster House was now the seat of the new Irish parliament. Discussions to remove the statue commenced in 1929 and the matter was frequently raised in parliamentary debates, but its removal did not begin until 1948. It took nearly eight weeks to dislodge the statue from its location and move it to storage in the Royal Hospital at Kilmainham, Dublin. The space occupied by the statue eventually became a car park for use by government ministers and civil servants.

In the 1950s, proposals were mooted to move the statue to Canada where such royal emblems of empire were still in favour. However, the transport costs were deemed to be too high. In the 1970s, as the hospital was renovated, the statue was firstly moved into a courtyard at the Royal Hospital before transportation to a disused reformatory, St. Conleth's in Daingean, County Offaly.

In 1986, after protracted negotiations, the statue was eventually sent to Australia. It now stands outside a shopping centre on Bicentennial Square in Sydney, where it bares the following inscription: 'At the request of the City of Sydney, this statue was presented by the Government and people of Ireland in a spirit of goodwill and friendship.' Some parts of the monument remain in Dublin: several cherubs are now situated in

the grounds of the Irish Museum of Modern Art at the Royal Hospital, Kilmainham, while *A Dying Irish Soldier Overlooked by Erin* is on the roof garden of the Dublin Castle conference centre, a location where public access is regulated.

An earlier statue of Victoria's husband, Prince Albert, is now the only remaining royal statue in Dublin and is located within the Leinster House complex. Despite a 2018 petition for its removal, the government decided that the statue should remain in situ.

OPPOSITE PAGE, LEFT AND BELOW The Queen Victoria statue in its original position on Leinster Lawn. The irony is that the statue was eventually transported to Australia, like so many of her subjects during her reign.

SLIEVEMORE VILLAGE, ACHILL ISLAND, COUNTY MAYO

ABANDONED 1948

This deserted village on Achill Island off County Mayo contains the now ruined remains of around eighty stone cottages. They stretch along the base of Slievemore, the second highest mountain on Ireland's largest offshore island. The name Slievemore is derived from the Irish name Sliabh Mór, which means great or big mountain.

It is thought that settlement in the area dates back to the Bronze Age. The houses in the village were occupied by farmers during the summer months when they herded their cattle from the lowlands to the highlands. Known as 'booley' or 'byre' houses

(from the Irish *buaile*, which translates as a 'milking place' or 'hill dwelling'), they were usually single-room cottages which were typically thatched with heather.

Booleying had advantages for the productivity of farms and small-holdings as it maintained the health of livestock and thus allowed for larger herds. This seasonal practice of moving livestock from one grazing area to another is also known as transhumance and it was continued on Achill island up to the early 1940s. Archive photos from this period, taken under the auspices of the Irish Folklore Commission, show the houses in the process of being thatched.

OPPOSITE PAGE Renewing the thatch on a Slievemore cottage in the 1940s.

BELOW An adjacent house abandoned and in ruins in 2017.

Around eighty-four houses remain out of the 137 that appear on the Ordnance Survey map of 1838. An archaeological summer school has been established on the island and it explores the earlier use of the site. Excavations and digs have revealed that the village includes three separate clusters of houses which were placed at a right-angle to the long street. No mortar or cement was used in their construction. It appears that the site was flexible, and during certain periods in the past the residents stayed all year round; for example, in the 19th century when farmers were evicted from their main holdings near the village of Dooagh. Some of the more complex house types in the village are viewed as indicators that the village was a permanent settlement. Oral histories gathered in the 20th century show that booleying was a fairly relaxed activity and that it was often undertaken by young children or older women.

The specific reasons behind the abandonment of the village are not known; however, the entire island had high rates of emigration, with Cleveland, Ohio, being a particular favoured destination. The availability of seasonal work in Scotland may also have been a factor. The last family to live in the village, the Callaghans, left in 1948 and emigrated to Scotland.

The concept of a deserted village has a deep resonance for many who visit the Achill site. This is in part due to the mass emigration from Ireland that occurred during the mid 19th century, when the Famine (1845–1849) caused a decline in the Irish population of a million through death and another million through emigration. A description of the village appeared in the German writer Heinrich Böll's bestselling *Irish Journal* (1957) in a chapter entitled 'Skeletons of a Human Habitation'. This influential book has done much to colour Germans' views of Ireland and it has sold over two million copies in Germany alone.

OPPOSITE PAGE When these photos were taken by the Irish Foklore Commission there was already a sense of documenting a vanishing way of life.

BELOW AND RIGHT How the row of cottages looks today. The village is regularly the study of historians investigating the economy of isolated rural communities.

ST. ANN'S HYDROPATHIC SPA, BLARNEY, CORK
CLOSED 1952

This institution was established by the Irish-born advocate of hydrotherapy Richard Barter in 1843. Situated on a raised site overlooking the River Shournagh, St. Ann's was a vast establishment that operated for over a hundred years. Its location was 2 miles (3 kilometres) from Blarney train station, thus connecting it to Cork and other cities via the extensive rail network.

Barter had requested the assistance of David Urquhart with his ideas for improvements on the Turkish bath. Urquhart, a Scottish politician and diplomat, was the chief promoter of Turkish baths and hydrotherapy in Britain. His book *Pillars of Hercules* (1850) attracted Barter's attention and formed the basis of his system, which he rolled out for the first time at St. Ann's. Barter had sent his nephew to Rome to study baths and as a result he devised what he called the Roman-Irish bath. In 1859 Barter took out a patent on the 'Improved Turkish Bath'. This method circulated dry air, which meant that the patients could tolerate higher temperatures, and it involved a series of plunges into hot and cold water. Similar Roman-

Irish baths were built throughout Ireland, and there were also examples in New York, Cape Town and Stockholm. His Irish establishments included two in Dublin – at the Hammam Family Hotel on O'Connell Street (destroyed in 1922 during the Civil War) and the Turkish baths on Lincoln Place (demolished in 1970).

St. Ann's was recommended as a winter residence for invalids, and the baths, fresh air and rest-cure were thought to aid a variety of ailments. The rest and relaxation on offer at such resorts were also marketed at the growing number of middle-class tourists, both Irish and British. Baths such as this became an important element of the Irish tourism experience.

During World War I it was requisitioned as a military hospital. Members of Barter's family continued to operate St. Ann's until 1952. Only the ruins of the complex remain today and it is gradually returning to nature. Plans to build a nursing home on the site were stalled when the owner of nearby Blarney Castle successfully halted the development. None of Dr Barter's baths survive in Ireland; however, some spas and resorts in Europe still apply his methods.

OPPOSITE PAGE In addition to the baths and therapy rooms St. Ann's boasted a library, billiards room (for both ladies and gentlemen), covered tennis courts and what was described as an American bowling alley. It had eighty guest rooms. A golf course was added to the facilities in 1907.

BELOW Contemporary accounts detail the oriental nature of the opulent interior design and the use of marble, mirrors and mosaics along with Cork red marble.

BOTTOM LEFT AND RIGHT Extensive manicured grounds led to woodland walks. The peak of popularity came between 1880 and 1920.

MEATH COUNTY GAOL, TRIM
DEMOLISHED 1953

The Meath County Gaol, located in the town of Trim, opened in 1834. Designed by John Hargrave and built around 1830, it was positioned on a prominent hill overlooking Trim Castle. This imposing building was designed along Jeremy Bentham's panopticon plan. Bentham was an English philosopher and social theorist whose template for prison layouts allowed all cells within an institution, to be observed by a single security guard. Thus the application of the word 'panopticon' which means all-seeing.

Trim Gaol has been the scene of some tragic incidents, and some of those associated with the institution have experienced tragedy. The architect of the building, John Hargrave, tragically drowned with all his family in Cardigan Bay, Wales, in 1833. His practice was based in Talbot Street, Dublin from 1826 until his death. Other buildings by Hargrave include gaols in Lifford, County Donegal, Omagh, County Tyrone, Mullingar, County Westmeath and in Longford town. He also undertook commissions for the design of courthouses.

It appears that the gaol was somewhat of a white elephant, as an inspector's report from the 1840s reveals that not all the cells were occupied due to a decline in criminality in the district. The inspector did note, however, that improvements could be made in the application of the 'separate' system which advocated the segregation of different classes of prisoners, the allocation of an individual cell to each prisoner, and the separating of prisoners during work hours. An annual report of 1870 shows that Trim gaol had four solitary cells and ninety-five other cells, plus two treadwheels. The report also suggests that Hargrave's design was not followed properly. Penal treadmills or wheels were used as a form of punishment for those who were sentenced to hard labour. Prisoners pedalled steps which were set in between iron wheels. Sometimes these efforts were used to pulp corn or raise water; however, in some prisons it was merely a futile exercise intended as punishment. It was known as 'grinding the wind'.

The building operated as a gaol until 1890 when it was then turned into an industrial school for pauper children. Then called the Trim Joint School, it had both a boys' and girls' section. Little remains by way of reports and overviews of the school's activities; however in 1912, John Kelly, an assistant teacher in the school, was killed in the schoolyard by a group of boys who were armed with brushes and sticks. The case resulted in a landmark trial which had implications for workmen's compensation. The arguments appear to have centred around whether or not Kelly's employers were liable for his death.

The bulk of the former prison was eventually demolished in 1953. During this demolition another tragedy struck when two men working on the site were killed. A reminder of the building can be found in the monumental 60-foot (18-metre) walls (pictured below), which are still intact. The remnants of the main entrance, built of rusticated limestone, are also particularly interesting and well built. In 2019, while working at the site for a new school, previously hidden cells and underground tunnels were discovered.

OPPOSITE PAGE The 1870 Prisons Report revealed that there were only twenty-eight people locked up in Trim Gaol in May of that year. The twenty-three men included one 'vagrant' and one 'criminal lunatic'. Of the five women incarcerated, three had been locked up for 'exposing or abandoning children'. The same report noted that only three men and one woman in Ireland received the death penalty in 1870.

GREAT BLASKET ISLAND, COUNTY KERRY
ABANDONED 1953

The now-abandoned Blasket Islands (Na Blascaodaí) are the most westerly islands in Europe and are situated several miles off the coast of Kerry. In the late 19th and early 20th centuries, residents were recognized by scholars, anthropologists and folklorists as the near last repository of traditional Irish customs and folklore. The islands were home to three celebrated writers in the Irish language: Tomás Ó Criomhthain, Peig Sayers and Muiris Ó Súilleabháin. Sayers' autobiography (which she dictated to her son Micheál) was on the curriculum in Irish secondary schools for many decades. It tells of her movement from the mainland upon marriage and the harshness of island life.

The Blasket Islands were a small fishing community and the population at the end of the 19th century was just under two hundred. This population had declined to twenty-two by the time the islands were evacuated in 1953. Many islanders emigrated to the United States, with Massachusetts being a favoured location. For example, Peig Sayers' six surviving children (she had eleven in total) all moved to America.

Protestant missionaries went to the islands in the late 1830s bringing with them biblical texts in Irish, and a Protestant school was built in 1839 but was derelict by 1880. The first photographs on Great Blasket were taken by Alma Curtin in 1892. Some of the cottages were built by the Congested Districts Board for Ireland, which was set up in 1891 to alleviate conditions on the western coast of Ireland. The village is on the east side of the island facing the mainland. The schoolhouse, which also served as a church, was built in 1864 and at one stage had sixty pupils.

It is believed that the playwright John Millington Synge used some of the islanders as inspiration for his controversial play *The Playboy of the Western World*. He visited the islands in 1905. Another visitor was Robin Flower, the English poet, translator and scholar who worked at the British Museum. Flower translated works from Irish including the writings of Tomás Ó Criomhthain. The scholar George Thomson had a role in publishing Muiris Ó Súilleabháin's *Fiche Bliain Ag Fás* (*Twenty Years A-Growing*) in 1933. Thomson, whose background was in classical scholarship, drew

parallels between the poets of the Blaskets and those of ancient Greece.

Great Blasket was inhabited until 1953 and its evacuation, following an extended period of bad weather when the island was cut off from the mainland, was a mournful event. Indeed, many felt that the government could have done more to support island life. In the 1980s the Taoiseach of Ireland, Charles Haughey, bought the smallest of the Blasket islands, Inishvickillane. An Blascaod Mór (Great Blasket) is now largely state owned and is visited by 10,000 people every year. In 2019, a job advert was posted looking for a couple to spend six months on the island as caretakers for three guest cottages and a coffee shop. They received over 24,000 applications.

TOP Gearóid Cheaist Ó Catháin, the last child on the island, photographed by the *Daily Mirror* in 1951.

ABOVE Stacking peat for drying in 1940.

OPPOSITE A view looking down on the village settlement on Great Blasket in 1940.

LHAMBRA
EASY TO LOVE
BLACK HORSE CANYON NAKED ALIBI
ALHAMBRA THEATRE
W.J. McMANUS & SON MOCCASINS
MAIN ENTRANCE TO ALL DEPARTMENTS

ALHAMBRA THEATRE, BELFAST
DEMOLISHED 1959

The Alhambra Theatre, located on Lower North Street, was first opened as a music hall in 1871. It was run by the comedian and impresario Dan Lowrey. The building was to fall victim to fires on three occasions over its history. The first incarnation of the building perished in flames and was rebuilt in 1873. The refurbished and improved theatre had many decorative features, including twelve star pendants, which hung from the main ceiling, and ornately decorated balconies. In 1879, the theatre was bought by another comedian, the flamboyant Irish-American William John Ashcroft. It had five bars to serve the two thousand customers it accommodated.

The theatre was refurbished in 1912 to a design by the architect William J. Moore with a French Renaissance style frontage. It became a full-time cinema in 1936, although it retained its licence to sell alcohol, thus making it a popular albeit rough and ready cinema that favoured Westerns and war movies. It was one of only two cinemas in Belfast that had an alcohol licence.

Fire struck again in December 1939 and this time only the front walls were left standing. The interior was redesigned by the province's best-known cinema architect, John McBride Neill, and reopened with a gala performance of films and variety acts in August 1940. The new theatre retained the existing facade but had a thoroughly modern interior. It was decorated with representations of Northern Ireland, such as Belfast and Strangford Lough, and Belfast's shipbuilding industry. A motto over the stage read 'Céad Míle Fáilte', which means 'one hundred thousand welcomes' in the Irish language. It boasted the most up-to-date sound equipment and facilities.

This photograph (left) was taken by Bert Hardy, best known for his contributions to the illustrated magazine *Picture Post*. The image was first published in June 1955 and shows the theatre's neon lettering shining in the evening light, evoking the atmosphere of a genteel time in the city prior to the outbreak of sectarian troubles.

The theatre was bought by the Rank Organisation in 1954 and was badly damaged by a fire which broke out in the balcony lounge of the cinema during a screening on the 10th of September 1959. At the time, around four hundred people were in the cinema and firemen reported that at first they had to encourage people to leave. The ceiling eventually fell through onto the auditorium, and the building was demolished later that year. The site is now occupied by a rather mundane office block called Temple Court.

OPPOSITE PAGE Bert Hardy's atmospheric photo for *Picture Post* taken in June, 1955.

RIGHT It became a cinema in 1936 and is shown here in 1937 with its French Renaissance frontage.

BELOW The original facade of the Alhambra with performances 'twice nightly'.

LIBERTY HALL, DUBLIN
DEMOLISHED 1959

Located on Beresford Place and Eden Quay on the northside of the River Liffey, Liberty Hall played an important role in the struggle for Irish independence. It became the headquarters of the Irish Transport and General Workers Union (I.T.G.W.U.) in 1912 when the union purchased the then derelict Northumberland Hotel. The hotel had been built in 1820 as part of a leisure complex that also included shops, a café and Turkish baths, which were accessible from Abbey Street. Liberty Hall became a hub for radical politics in the years leading up to the 1916 Rising and provided a meeting place for many groups, including the Irish Women Workers' Union. During the 1913 Dublin Lock-out (a bitter industrial dispute that lasted for six months) Liberty Hall acted as a soup kitchen and it was the location from which strike pay was distributed. It then became the headquarters of the Irish Citizen Army, a small group established to defend striking workers whose members subsequently played a role in the 1916 Rising. In the period immediately prior to the Rising it was used to store ammunition and weapons.

A printing press was located in the basement of the hall and it was from here that James Connolly published his weekly newspaper, *The Workers' Republic*, between 1915 and 1916. 'The 1916 Proclamation of the Irish Republic', one of the most iconic documents of Irish history, was also printed in the building. The hall was raided by the military and hit and damaged by bombardment during the Rising. However, it dodged the fires which ravaged other city centre buildings and was restored.

Despite its place in Irish history, the building was demolished in the late 1950s to make way for the modern Liberty Hall. Construction on the new International-style tower began in 1961 and at sixteen storeys high was the first high-rise building in Dublin city centre.

OPPOSITE PAGE Liberty Hall was built as the Northumberland Hotel and Coffee House before it was bought by the Irish Transport and General Workers' Union. It is pictured here as Liberty Hall with a parade of the Irish Citizen Army in 1914.

FAR LEFT Unlike many buildings in the Easter Rising, Liberty Hall escaped long-term damage.

LEFT Liberty Hall in the 1930s.

BELOW The modern office block that replaced Liberty Hall is still Dublin's tallest skyscraper.

MOTE PARK HOUSE, COUNTY ROSCOMMON

REBUILT AFTER 1866 FIRE, DEMOLISHED 1959

During the 19th century, fire was a constant threat to the country houses of the landed gentry in Ireland, and Mote Park House, Ballymurray, the seat of the Crofton family, was one such casualty. On the 20th of May 1866, the neoclassical mansion, designed by the architect Richard Morrison, was engulfed by flames. Local newspapers reported the valiant attempts made by tenants to save the house, but while many of the contents were retrieved the house was destroyed.

It appears that the Crofton estate was in healthy financial standing in the decades after the Famine and Lord Crofton had the wherewithal to rebuild immediately. Making alterations to Morrison's original design, he employed the best of Irish craftsmen and sourced materials from around the world. The newly restored house was described by Mark Bence Jones as having 'a nine-bay entrance front with a three-bay pedimented breakfront, with a single storey Ionic portico'. It included twenty marble mantelpieces and panels in Honduras mahogany; an oval library with tripartite windows opened onto the manicured gardens.

The Croftons had a relatively benign relationship with their tenants; nonetheless, the social changes of the 19th century meant that there was a transfer of land ownership from landlord to tenant. This continued with the newly independent Ireland and by the mid 20th century only 700 acres (283 hectares) of the original 7,000 remained in the family's ownership.

Eventually the house and estate were transferred to the state. Roscommon County Council decided that the rates were too onerous to pay so they removed the roof of the house and it was demolished in 1959.

The component parts of Mote Park House were dispersed during the demolition process and their location remains unknown; however, a surprising lot turned up in a sale in 2015. The reclaimed portico of the house was auctioned for €12,000 as part of the sale of Kedagh Park in County Galway. It had been rescued at the time of demolition by the collector Father Brian Hanley.

The Croftons were keen botanists and the parkland surrounding their home was landscaped with many ornamental structures. Fine native groves contained great oaks along with beech, ash and hazel. The grounds remain an attraction for local walkers and some of the original landscaping and ornamental features endure. The Irish Georgian Society facilitated the recent restoration of the James Gandon-designed Lion Gate, which rests on a Doric triumphal arch, and it is indicative of the craftsmanship and taste of the original owners.

OPPOSITE PAGE Anyone for tennis? A house party of the Crofton family poses for the camera on the rear lawn.

LEFT A view of the front of the house at Mote Park. As noted above, the portico was sold on.

BELOW Mote Park's original Lion Gate has survived demolition and the Irish Georgian Society restored it in 2016.

RAILWAY STATION. KILKEE. 4220. W.L.

WEST CLARE NARROW-GAUGE RAILWAY

CLOSED 1961

The West Clare narrow gauge railway ran between Ennis, County Clare and Cappa/Kilrush Pier on the Shannon Estuary. The railway operated between 1887 and 1961 with numerous stops along the west coast of the county passing through rugged and beautiful landscape. Stops included the seaside town of Lahinch and the market town of Ennistymon. It also stopped at smaller hamlets and villages and at one stage there was even a private stop at Lahinch Workhouse. The railway line was notorious for delays and poor timekeeping and was the subject of a well-known song by Percy French entitled *Are Ye Right There, Michael? Are Ye Right?* which humorously mocked the tardiness associated with the railway.

It was hoped that the introduction of this railway line would benefit the depressed economies located on the west coast of Ireland. Narrow-gauge tracks were cheaper to build and this meant that the project was viable and could offer better returns for investors. Railways in the 19th century were run by private companies, and the county of Clare had two: the West Clare Railway and the South Clare Railway, but these were eventually merged. Stops varied from fine stone-built stations to single platforms with small wooden waiting shelters.

Use of the railway was seasonal, with over two-thirds of the passengers travelling in the summer months. It was considered to be a great boon to the tourism industry, bringing visitors to events such as the Lisdonvarna Festival, the Kilrush Horse Fair and the Lahinch Garland Day. The latter took place on the last Sunday of July and was a celebration of the harvest with a carnival atmosphere. The railway also benefited agriculture, facilitating the transportation of cattle from the Burren. As it grew in popularity the service was increased to five trips per day and it was estimated that at its peak over 200,000 trips were taken per annum.

In 1925 the company was merged into Great Southern Railways. Services were reduced during World War II due to coal shortages; in general the decade of the 1940s was a trying time for railways, and many lines were closed. Government policy pushed people towards car ownership, and population loss in the region further compounded their decline.

Steam engines were eventually replaced by diesel engines. West Clare was the last narrow-gauge railway in Ireland to offer a passenger service and it finally closed in 1961, after which most of the track was taken up and the land was sold off. From the mid 1990s onwards steps were taken to reopen the railway line and part of the track has been given a new lease of life. The feasibility of making the railway into a walking trail or greenway has been explored; however, much of the route is now occupied by housing and access rights to farmland would prove problematic. Fine stations such as Kilrush no longer have their platforms or ancillary buildings. Others have completely disappeared; for example, Lahinch Station is now the site of a housing estate.

OPPOSITE PAGE The terminus at Kilkee. The West Clare line was three feet (91 centimetres) wide, while standard gauge was five feet and three inches (160 centimetres).

BELOW LEFT A specially built railcar pictured at Kilrush Station in the 1950s.

BELOW The restored booking hall in Moyasta Station with a prominent 1899 advertisement for an excursion to Kilkee.

THEATRE ROYAL, BELFAST
DEMOLISHED 1961

Belfast's Theatre Royal had several iterations in its 168 year history. The first theatre at the Arthur Street location (also known as the Arthur Street Theatre) operated between 1793 and 1871, the second between 1871 and 1881, and the third between 1881 and 1915.

The architects of the second Theatre Royal (below) were Lanyon, Lynn & Lanyon and they included carvings by the Fitzpatrick Brothers. Thomas and William Fitzpatrick were active between the 1850s and 1890s. They were also building contractors and their medallions, which adorned the front of the theatre, featured actors and actresses. The interior of the theatre contained Shakespearean scenes painted by Thomas Goodman. The first theatre was destroyed by fire in June 1881 and reopened in December the same year. This time the interior was redesigned by Charles Phipps whose first large-scale project was the Theatre Royal in Bath. He was also responsible for the Gaiety Theatre in Dublin.

Reporters noted that it had five separate entrances and this ensured that the various classes of patrons did not have to mingle with each other. In many ways the arrangement of the theatre reflected the hierarchical nature of the Victorian society. Stalls, boxes, circles and various galleries segregated the theatre's patrons.

The mosaics in the theatre's interior were by the Venetian company of Salviati and Burke. The chairs were described as being Phipps' own patented armchairs, which guaranteed comfort. The ceiling was painted with Italian Renaissance ornament and the red wallpaper was complemented by turquoise silk tapestries.

The productions at the Theatre Royal were varied and included operas, comedies, dramas, tragedies and musicals. The famous music hall singer Ida Barr made her debut there in 1898. Oscar Wilde gave two lectures at the venue on the 1st and 2nd of January 1884. The subjects of his lectures were: 'The House Beautiful' on the principles of decorative art as applied to the

home, and 'Personal Impressions of America', which was based on his year-long journey to that country.

In 1895, the programme included productions of *The Bohemian Girl* by the Irish composer Michael William Balfe and comic opera *The Marriage of Figaro*. The Carl Rosa Opera Company also performed in that year. During this period Nita Carritte toured as the company's prima donna. Other notable performers included Henry Irving, the famous actor-manager, who performed *Faust* in 1902, and another actor-manager, Frank Benson, who appeared in Belfast on a regular basis.

Due to the public's changing entertainment tastes the theatre eventually was converted into the Royal Cinema, with the last theatrical performance taking place in March 1915. It was substantially remodelled by the well-known theatre/cinema architect Bertie Crewe during this period.

The cinema was demolished in 1961. A four-storey post-modern building was built on the site in the 1960s. It is currently a Starbucks coffee shop, although there are several redevelopment proposals on the table, which would result in the demolition of the building.

OPPOSITE PAGE AND LEFT Two images of the third Theatre Royal. By the time of its closure as a performance venue in 1915 it had lost the Palladian frieze.

FAR LEFT Although rudimentary in appearance, this was the second Theatre Royal on the site, dating from 1871 to 1881, when it was destroyed by that perennial menace to theatres — fire.

SAILORTOWN, BELFAST
DISMANTLED 1960s

Sailortown was a working-class community in North Belfast made up of both Protestant and Catholic dockworkers, living in closely packed terraced housing and working nearby. When Belfast was a centre of linen manufacture and engineering, almost two thousand worked in and around the docks, and added to that mix were visiting sailors from across Europe – especially the Baltic states. At the end of the 19th century Italian immigrants settled around Little Patrick Street adding to the varied make-up of the residents.

The spiritual needs of the community were addressed by two prominent churches on Corporation Street; Sinclair Seamen's Presbyterian Church and St. Joseph's Roman Catholic Church (1880). Sinclair Seamen's Presbyterian Church was opened in 1857 and designed by Charles Lanyon, the architect responsible for several well-known Belfast buildings including Queen's University, Belfast. The church had a maritime theme with a wooden pulpit shaped like a ship's prow.

In World War II the Luftwaffe bombed key docklands in London, Liverpool and Swansea, and despite the distance, Belfast was not exempt. In April and May of 1941 many buildings in Sailortown were hit with incendiaries. The large York Street Spinning Mill was engulfed in flames and one of its walls crushed adjacent houses in Vere and Sussex streets. The 1898 Midland Hotel was also destroyed in the Blitz and subsequently rebuilt in 1948.

In the 1960s, the building of the M2 motorway displaced many families who were then moved to newly built housing estates on the outskirts of the city. Many of the residential streets were demolished, for example, Trafalgar Street which once had sixty

houses was razed to make way for the motorway. Just four of the original houses on Garmoyle Street remain standing. Although the area did have its share of deprivation and sectarianism, the loss of cobbled streets like Pilot Street and Ship Street and the dispersal of populations to suburban housing estates had a terminal effect on Sailortown. The lack of a viable congregation led to St Joseph's deconsecration by the Diocese of Down and Connor in 2001. Although there has been much redevelopment in the area, the sense of an identifiable community disappeared in the 1960s at the hands of urban planners.

RIGHT St. Joseph's Roman Catholic Church.

BELOW The nautical-themed pulpit of Sinclair Seamen's Presbyterian Church. A rare survivor of Sailortown's past.

OPPOSITE PAGE TOP A photo looking down Corporation Street towards Garmoyle Street. The Italianate tower on the right belongs to the Sinclair Seamen's Church. Today this view is bisected by a motorway overpass.

OPPOSITE PAGE LEFT Madden Brothers' warehouse stood at the corner of Whitla and Garmoyle streets.

OPPOSITE PAGE RIGHT The 1948 Midland Hotel photographed in the late 1950s.

ORIGINAL ABBEY THEATRE, DUBLIN
DEMOLISHED 1961

The Abbey Theatre, which hosts the National Theatre of Ireland, first opened in 1904. It is credited with being one of the first state-subsidized theatres in the world and it has received an annual government grant since 1925. It has its origins in the Irish Literary Revival which looked to the country's Gaelic past and heightened national identity. The theatre set out to promote the works of Irish playwrights and to employ Irish actors while also looking to developments in Europe.

Englishwoman Annie Horniman and the director William Fay had bought the Mechanics Theatre and nearby buildings on Abbey Street in Dublin's North Inner City in order to put on plays by the Irish National Theatre Society. W. B. Yeats, Lady Gregory and John Millington Synge were instrumental in this early incarnation and the first play was put on in December 1904. The building was adapted by Joseph Holloway and included Arts and Craft elements and stained glass by Sarah Purser.

A civil disturbance took place at the theatre in 1907 when John Millington Synge staged his play *The Playboy of the Western World* which outraged the audience who believed that use of the word 'shift' was derogatory to Irish women. Known as the 'playboy riots' they were stoked by nationalists who also felt that the theatre was not political enough. The managers of the theatre fell out with Annie Horniman and with the loss of her financial support the theatre was in a precarious state.

The plays of Sean O'Casey, starting with *The Shadow of a Gunman* (1923), revived its fortunes. However, his play *The Plough and the Stars* (1926) also caused riots and he left for England soon after. In 1927, the Peacock Theatre opened its doors to showcase more experimental plays on a smaller stage in an annex to the Abbey. A ballet school was established in 1928 and was lead by the Irish-born dancer Dame Ninette de Valois.

The original building was destroyed by fire in 1951 and was demolished in 1961. The Dublin City architect Daithí Hanly saved the granite blocks which made up the facade of the building. Following the fire, the Abbey was based in the Queen's Theatre for fifteen years. A new building was designed by the architects Ronald Tallon and Michael Scott (a former Abbey Theatre actor). The building was a windowless modernist cube in grey brick, which is scheduled to be replaced.

OPPOSITE PAGE AND ABOVE The original Abbey Theatre was an intimate and influential performance space. After rioting in 1926 at Sean O'Casey's *The Plough and the Stars*, W. B. Yeats famously railed against the rioters: 'You have disgraced yourself again. Is this to be the recurring celebration of Irish genius? Synge first and then O'Casey.

RIGHT The original replacement Abbey Theatre photographed in the 1960s. It subsequently had a large, modern portico added to break up the expanse of wall. In January 2020 it was announced that after only fifty years' use Scott and Tallon's building will be mostly demolished.

ROSAPENNA HOTEL, COUNTY DONEGAL
BURNED 1962

Opened in May 1893, this wooden hotel building was atypical for Ireland. It was designed in Sweden and made from Norwegian pine which had been shipped to the remote location in north-west Donegal. Robert B. Clements, the 4th Earl of Leitrim, was the visionary behind the hotel, but never got to see his vision realized. He died of blood poisoning in 1892, a couple of months after his return from Sweden where he had purchased the wood to build the hotel.

Located on the remote shores of Sheephaven Bay, close to a private 3-mile sandy beach, it offered bathing, boating, lawn tennis and croquet. Fresh and saltwater angling were also an attraction with free access to rivers on the earl's estates. During this period the county of Donegal was promoted as 'Norway in Ireland'.

It was an attempt to reconstruct the image of the county, which was viewed as wild and inhospitable, prone to civil unrest and poor standards of hygiene. These marketing efforts were generally directed towards the British tourist market and they emphasized the cleanliness of the facilities.

The unusual design combined features of Norwegian Inns and Swiss chalets. The yellow and black exterior had a first floor veranda and many of the small but airy bedrooms had French windows leading to balconies. Each bedroom had its own bathroom and the hotel also had central heating. Dragon heads adorned the front of the building and the Scandinavian motif was continued inside as the ironwork and locks on guest bedrooms were Norwegian in theme. The hotel employed German waiters, who added to the continental ambiance of the resort. Billiards, smoking

OPPOSITE PAGE AND ABOVE The Rosapenna Hotel was one of the first purpose-built golf hotels. Scottish golfer and course architect Old Tom Morris started work on the links course two years before the hotel opened.

RIGHT Guests enjoy sea views from the first floor veranda.

and reading rooms were available to the guests and offered recreation on wet days.

The hotel's construction marked the beginning of Ireland's ascendancy as a golfing destination. Rosapenna Hotel would be promoted as a golf resort, one of the world's first. In 1891, Old Tom Morris (Thomas Mitchell Morris), the famous Scottish golfer and course designer, had been invited to create an 18-hole golf course for the hotel. In 1901 the hotel even had a resident professional golfer, the Derry-born Joe Harvey.

The earl's successor, Charles Clements, continued the development of the hotel and mortgaged his estates to help pay for future developments, but it never quite prospered. A weekly steamboat service from Derry and Glasgow was introduced to make Rosapenna more accessible to visitors, but it proved difficult to get a return on the investment.

The hotel closed during World War I and reopened in 1924. In 1940 it was sold to Howard Catherwood of Belfast. In the same year the railway station at Cresslough closed and this, combined with World War II, saw a parlous decline in business. Destroyed by fire in 1962, there is now a new hotel on the site and its emphasis is very much on the golfing heritage, with a Harry Vardon restaurant.

OPPOSITE PAGE Courteous diners and waiters pause for a long exposure photograph of the dining room.

ABOVE LEFT The Rosapenna entertained golfing royalty in 1906. Six-times Open Champion Harry Vardon (seated bottom left) came to the Rosapenna to improve the design of the course by adding more length to the holes and more bunkers.

TOP Apart from the excellent 18-hole golf course; a tennis court and a billiards room were obligatory additions to any upmarket Victorian hotel.

ABOVE Famous visitors to the old Rosapenna included John Wayne and Errol Flynn, but the hotel was beyond redemption after the fire. The new Rosapenna is a modern complex.

THEATRE ROYAL, DUBLIN

Will Artistes please note that in the interests of stage efficiency, any friends or persons not employed in the Theatre "must not" in any circumstances be taken on to the stage without the permission of

STAGE MANAGER

THEATRE ROYAL, DUBLIN

DEMOLISHED 1962

The Theatre Royal is a popular name and indeed Dublin has had no less than five establishments with this title. Opened in 1897 on Hawkins Street, the fourth Theatre Royal was designed by Frank Matcham and was built on the site of the Leinster Hall Theatre, which itself had been built on the site of the third Theatre Royal.

Edward VII attended a state performance at the theatre in April 1904 along with a capacity audience of 2,011. Switching from opera and musical comedy to a more popular music hall variety bill, in 1906 a young Charlie Chaplin trod the boards at the Royal as part of The Eight Lancashire Lads. In the late 1920s and early 1930s it was converted to a cinema and finally closed on the 3rd of March 1934.

The fifth and final Royal was a large Art Deco entertainment complex. Built in 1934 it had a capacity of 3,700. Its lavish interior had a Moorish theme, referencing the Alhambra, while its exterior boasted modern streamlining and neon. The floodlit facade was adorned with sculptured figures. Its architect, Leslie Morton, created a truly modern palace of entertainment, escape and fantasy replete with cinemas, bars and restaurants.

The Royal had a resident 25-piece orchestra and was essentially a place for variety entertainment, hosting acts such as George Formby as well as home-grown talent. The annual Christmas pantomime filled the auditorium for weeks.

The Royalettes were the theatre's chorus girls (modelled on the Rockettes, at New York's Radio City Music Hall) and were the epitome of glamour and style. Big international stars performed there over the years, including Judy Garland, Nat King Cole, Bob Hope and Bill Haley and the Comets.

The adjoining Regal Rooms were built on the site of the Winter Gardens and were a place for wining and dining. Heralded as a cosmopolitan and sophisticated rendezvous in the opening programme, the Theatre Royal complex included several bars whose names conjured up a world of elegance: the Marine Bar had Australian walnut and black beam timbering and was situated underground, hence its nickname the Submarine Bar. The Upper Circle Bar offered more refined dining and drinking amid velvet and red leather sofas. The Tea Lounge offered light refreshments in a room decorated in a rose-pink palette.

The death of the variety circuit coupled with competition from television precipitated the theatre's decline. Some argued that such a large venue was never really viable in a city of Dublin's size.

The Theatre Royal closed its doors on the 30th of June 1962 and was demolished soon after to make way for Hawkins House, a twelve-storey modern office block which housed the Department of Health. Designed by Thomas Bennett, it was voted the ugliest building in Dublin. In 2016 plans were unveiled for its demolition and a total redevelopment of the site. At the time of writing this had not yet happened.

OPPOSITE PAGE The *Irish Independent* newspaper sent a photographer to record the last day of the Theatre Royal and gathered the staff together for a photo on a side street.

LEFT The final Theatre Royal was a large Art Deco entertainment complex.

FITZWILLIAM STREET LOWER, DUBLIN
DEMOLISHED 1964

In 1961, the Electricity Supply Board of Ireland (ESB) announced its intention to demolish a run of sixteen townhouses which formed part of an unbroken, half-mile-long parade of Georgian dwellings in Dublin. The terrace of late-18th-century houses, which ran from Merrion Square to Fitzwilliam Place, were to be razed to make way for the Board's new headquarters.

The Palladian-derived architecture of Georgian Dublin was elegant and balanced. The facades of these buildings were symmetrical with classical dimensions and multi-paned long windows. Although the panelled doors were generally painted in a uniform dark grey colour, they were often topped with ornate fanlights. It was in the interiors of these houses where the owners expressed their taste and individuality. They often contained the work of Irish and Italian artisans who decorated the ceilings with elaborate stucco works, and living and drawing rooms boasted beautiful marble fireplaces. Within the house the typical layout included a *piano nobile* on the first floor, which contained the main reception rooms of the house.

During this period there was little sympathy for Georgian architecture in Ireland, with many perceiving it as a legacy of the British Empire; this despite the fact that the houses were commissioned, built and decorated by Irish craftsmen. By the 1960s many of the townhouses had become slum or tenement buildings, which were allowed to decline.

In 1962, the competition to design the energy company's headquarters was won by the controversial young architect Sam Stephenson who, along with his partner Arthur Gibney, ran a fashionable Dublin practice, and who was also responsible for the controversial Wood Quay development, as well as the design of the iconic Central Bank on Dame Street. Stephenson argued that Georgian buildings were never intended to last more than a lifetime.

The announcement of plans to demolish the houses was met with protest by groups such as the Irish Georgian Society, and a bitter battle ensued with many protests and meetings. The ESB contended that the buildings were structurally unsound and of no architectural interest. It was noted that the company itself had already hollowed out much of the original interior features during their decades-long tenure on the street. Some architectural students demonstrated in favour of the scheme and many of the leading politicians saw little worthy of preservation.

On the 20th of December 1964, the day before new planning legislation was due to come into force, permission was granted to demolish the houses. They were taken down in the summer of 1965. It is widely believed that their demolition heralded the destruction of much of Georgian Dublin.

In 2017, the ESB announced that it was about to redevelop its headquarters and its intention to demolish the Stephenson building. It was taken down in 2018, having stood for just over fifty years.

OPPOSITE PAGE AND BELOW The buildings were demolished in 1965 despite public protest.

NELSON'S PILLAR, DUBLIN

1966

This monument to Britain's naval commander at the Battle of Trafalgar, Horatio Nelson, stood on Dublin's main thoroughfare Sackville (later O'Connell) Street from 1809 until it was blown up in 1966. The landmark was initially designed by William Wilkins and greatly modified by Francis Johnston.

The large granite pillar was visible throughout the city and was topped by a statue of Nelson sculpted by Thomas Kirk. The four sides of the pedestal were engraved with Nelson's greatest victories, namely St. Vincent, the Nile, Copenhagen and Trafalgar. A spiral stairway of 168 steps filled the interior of the column, leading to a viewing platform just beneath the statue. For a fee, you could climb to the top and gain a panoramic view of both the city and Dublin Bay. Alterations were made in 1894, which created a new entrance to the stairway, and the entire pillar was surrounded by iron railings. Nelson's Pillar was the terminus for many of the Dublin City tram routes.

From the late 19th century onwards nationalist sentiment rose and Nelson's presence on Dublin's main street became increasingly contentious. During the Easter Rising in 1916 an attempt was purportedly made to blow up the pillar, but the explosives failed to ignite due to dampness (though this Easter Rising episode is disputed by some). In 1955, a group of

OPPOSITE PAGE Admiral Horatio Nelson gazes down Sackville Street, past the General Post Office, towards the river Liffey.

BELOW Nelson's Pillar was the terminus for many tram services, but also the site for many flower stalls.

University College Dublin students broke into the pillar, hung up a poster of the college's revolutionary former student Kevin Barry and attempted to melt the statue with a flamethrower – all to no avail. The names of the students were taken by the guards, though none of them were prosecuted.

Fifty years after the Easter Rising, the monument was finally destroyed by an explosion on the 8th of March 1966. The Army were called in to fully demolish the stump by controlled explosion several days later.

The destruction was masterminded by a group of young Republicans; however, it wasn't until 2000, that Liam Sutcliffe fully revealed the story of how he planted the bomb. Local businesses received compensation for minor damage and loss of earnings and the site passed into the ownership of the Dublin Corporation.

Later in 1966 Nelson was again the victim of student high jinks when his disembodied head was stolen form a Corporation storage yard by a group of students from the National College of Art and Design. In a nod to the antics of the existentialist Theatre of the Absurd, the students took the head to London, and he also made a stage appearance with the folk band The Dubliners. In the end the head was returned to the Dublin Corporation where it entered the collection of the Dublin Civic Museum. It is now in the custody of the Dublin City Archives and Library.

The pillar was eventually replaced by Ian Ritchie's *Spire of Dublin*, also known as the Monument of Light, or by its Irish name of *An Túr Solais*. The plain, stainless steel, mast-like structure is 120 metres (390 feet) in height and was unveiled in 2003. During the construction phase, archaeologists uncovered the remains of the first buildings on the site in the form of the cellars of 17th-century Dutch Billy-style houses.

OPPOSITE PAGE *Picture Post* cameraman Bert Hardy took this photo looking up what was now O'Connell Street towards Nelson's Pillar in 1955.

ABOVE RIGHT The bomb-blasted stump attracted great crowds to the city centre in 1966.

RIGHT Two members of the Garda recover Nelson's head, which was to enjoy more travel in the future.

FAR RIGHT Given the number of British statues removed by the Irish Free State it was perhaps surprising it had lasted so long.

THE IRISH HOUSE, DUBLIN

DEMOLISHED 1969

This unusual public house was located on Wood Quay on the south side of the River Liffey at the corner of Wood Quay and Winetavern Street. Set against the backdrop of Christ Church Cathedral, Winetavern Street was traditionally the location for public houses. The exterior of the Irish House was decorated with colourful stucco work by William Burnet and John Comerford. The subjects adorning the building were nationalist and neo-Celtic in design and theme, and they included life-size figures of Daniel O'Connell, Henry Grattan and members of the Irish parliament. A full tableau depicts Henry Grattan's last address to the Irish parliament and features seventeen wig-wearing politicians.

In addition to these figures, the facade was decorated with many of the historic symbols and emblems of Ireland, such as harps, round towers and Irish wolfhounds (of which there were six). Built in 1870 for P. P. Kelly, the public house was later owned by the O'Meara family and by S. Timoney in the 1930s. The names of the publicans were inscribed in a beautiful Gaelic script in gilt paint. Burnet and Comerford were also responsible for the ornate designs on the Oarsman public house in the Ringsend part of the city.

The pub appears in the film adaptation of James Joyce's novel *Ulysses* staring Milo O'Shea, which was made on location in Dublin in 1967. It also features in Flora Mitchell's book *Vanishing Dublin* (1966), which reproduced her watercolour over pen and ink depictions of the city in a time of change.

The pub was demolished to make way for the Dublin Corporation offices designed by the controversial architect Sam Stephenson. The location at Wood Quay had been the site of an early Viking settlement, deemed to be one of the most important sites in Europe, and also contained a long section of the medieval city walls. The public attempted to halt the development and in September 1978, 20,000 people marched through the streets of Dublin requesting that the site be made a national monument. There were then several court cases in which archaeologists and conservationists made the case for the site's retention, but all to no avail. The first phase of Stephenson's design was built between 1980 and 1985.

A portion of the city walls were preserved in the basement of the new offices. Between 1974 and 1981 extensive archaeological digs took place on the site and the objects found at Wood Quay are now in the collection of the National Museum of Ireland. Lord Moyne, of the Guinness Brewery, had earlier financed a project to salvage the exterior of the Irish House, and the stucco figures were retrieved from the building in 1968 and moved to the Guinness Museum. They are now in the care of the Dublin Civic Trust.

OPPOSITE PAGE The Irish House photographed in 1965.

ABOVE AND LEFT Despite a large protest, the site was redeveloped; however the exterior facade and figures were saved and preserved by the Guinness Museum.

OUTDOOR HANDBALL ALLEYS

RULE CHANGE 1969

Outdoor handball alleys were once commonplace throughout Ireland. Handball Is a game where players hit a ball against a wall with their hands, attempting to prevent the other player or players from returning serve. It can be played in singles or doubles.

The earliest recorded purpose-built handball alleys were constructed in Ireland in the 1790s. In the first few decades of the newly independent Ireland there was a boom in the building of the alleys. Wholesome outdoor activities such as handball played a role in the building of national identity within the new state. While the sport of cricket was now shunned, the government considered other sports favourably as they were free to use and offered an alternative to drinking alcohol in public houses. Handball alleys were places for social gatherings and acted as a focal point for the community.

These three- or four-walled courts are recognized as a vernacular building type that is unique to Ireland. Usually rendered in cement, there were many regional variations with regard to wall size and dimensions. Unadorned and functional, their appearance was governed by the constructs of the game; however, each was unique with regard to its setting and surroundings. Some included a viewing platform or tiered stands. Some were built by the community or attached to schools, colleges, barracks or public institutions. Courts were also built by Irish communities abroad.

The photograph above right shows two unnamed handball players who took part in the 1928 Tailteann Games. These games took place between 1924 and 1932 and were an annual event highlighting Irish sports. Taking inspiration from ancient games and gatherings the competition provided positivity in the wake of the turmoil of the Civil War.

Foreign nationals of Irish descent could also participate in the games and it was felt that this would also boost the tourist industry.

Irish emigrants introduced handball to their new host countries, particularly during the 19th century when Irish emigration to America was at its highest. Two of the earliest handball alleys were constructed in San Francisco in 1873, and Phil Casey (a world

champion handball player who emigrated to New York) built a four-walled court at Degraw Street, Brooklyn, in 1882. Casey was at the forefront of popularizing the sport in New York and during this period the games attracted large crowds and high prize monies.

With new global interest in the sport, international rules began to dominate, and the adoption of the international standard in 1969 led to the decline of outdoor courts. The original Gaelic rules had been drawn up in 1884, but new rules required the use of a soft rubber ball rather than the 'Irish hardball', and the court size was reduced to 20 by 40 feet (6 by 12 metres), making the old outside courts redundant.

There are currently 900 alleys in Ireland, many dating from the heyday of handball and many in poor repair due to the sport's decline and preferences for indoor courts not affected by the elements.

OPPOSITE PAGE A school handball alley in the 1930s.

ABOVE Handball is still played, but these days indoors. Kells Handball Club was set up in 1985.

ABOVE LEFT Two players pose for the camera at the 1928 Tailteann Games. The Games have an ancient history dating back to before the Norman Invasion of Ireland. They are said to have three functions: honouring ancestors, proclaiming laws, and the gathering to play games and celebrate.

PICTUREDROME CINEMA, BELFAST
CLOSED 1970

The Picturedrome in East Belfast was designed by John McBride Neill, the leading cinema architect in Northern Ireland. He was responsible for many spectacular cinemas including the Apollo, the Tonic in Bangor, the New Vic in Belfast and the Ritz in Ballybofey, County Donegal. He designed six cinemas in 1935 alone!

There had been a cinema (also called the Picturedrome) on the site at Mountpottinger Road from 1911, though this was destroyed by fire and demolished in 1934. The new Picturedrome reopened on the 10th of November 1934 with a gala performance in aid of Templemore Avenue hospital. Its Art Deco facade and interiors were decorated using a chevron motif. It was devoid of the fussy ornamentation that characterized earlier cinema interiors. Its gleaming white facade was augmented with green and red neon lettering and this made it stand out, especially at night, against the rows of redbrick houses and shops.

The foyer led to two luxury lounges and it had 1,000 seats divided between the ground floor and a large balcony. The overall palette was in gold and sand and the cinema seats were upholstered in a rich blue velvet. The interior used modern materials such as glass bricks, light boxes, monochrome tiles and polished floors. Modern steel furniture and tubular light fittings were used in the two lounge areas. These also had velvet-covered seats and abstract patterned carpets. Overall, it conveyed a sense of luxury and glamour that was devoid in the surrounding terraces.

In the 1930s, the programme at the Picturedrome changed three times per week with new films being shown on Mondays, Wednesdays and Fridays. The film on show when these photographs were taken was *The Masquerader* which was originally released in 1933.

These photographs are part of the Alexander R. Hogg Collection which is now in the collection of the National Museums of Northern Ireland. Hogg was a professional studio photographer who undertook commissions for a wide variety of organizations, including the City Council and architectural firms. He worked in Belfast until the late 1930s.

It was not the only Picturedrome in the city. There was a much smaller Shankill Picturedrome on the

corner of Shankill Road and Northumberland Avenue, run by 'Wee Joe' McKibben, which started up in 1910 and lasted until 1958.

The larger Picturedrome was owned by a Mr. P. Pounds from 1947; however, it was bought by the Rank Organisation in 1955, which ran the cinema until its closure on the 30th of May 1970.

The Art Deco building was demolished in the 1990s and a housing scheme was put in its place. Unfortunately, The Strand in Belfast is the only one of John McBride Neill's cinemas that is still in working order and, indeed, most were demolished or had a change of use during his lifetime.

OPPOSITE PAGE The Picturedrome on Mountpottinger Road in 1934.

TOP AND ABOVE The foyer and upstairs lounge area of the Picturedrome, which vied with the Troxy and the Lido on Shore Road for customers.

OLD BRIDGE. BIRR. KINGS Co. 9953. W.L.

OLD BRIDGE, BIRR, COUNTY OFFALY
HOUSES DEMOLISHED 1971

Birr is a small town located in the midlands county of Offaly. It was also known as Parsonstown in reference to the local landowning family, the Parsons, and it retains many of its Georgian features. Formally laid out along wide streets, it includes a square centred around an obelisk and a mall called Oxmantown Mall, which leads to Birr Castle.

The castle is the home of the Parsons family and the Earls of Rosse and is one of the oldest inhabited homes in Ireland. It was the site of The Leviathan, or Rosse 6-foot (1.8-metre) telescope, which was the largest telescope in the world from 1845 until 1917. Birr Castle was also the home of Mary, Countess of Rosse, an early practitioner of photography and a keen amateur astronomer. Her original darkroom is preserved at the castle.

The Old Bridge at Birr was built around 1660 and spanned the River Camcor, a tributary of the Little Brosna River. This four-arched bridge was the only bridge in County Offaly upon which houses were built. These unusual dwellings, some of which were three storeys, were constructed without foundations and with water flowing beneath them.

A history of the town of Birr by Thomas Lalor Cooke published in 1875 refers to a flood which took place in the town on the 12th of November 1787 during which the river rose to an unprecedented height. It states that the water level was recorded on the oak staircase of one of the houses on the bridge where a mark and inscription showed that the water rose more than 7 feet (2 metres) over the its usual height.

The photograph at left was most probably taken from the nearby Manor Mill, by Robert French for the Dublin firm of William Lawrence. This atmospheric and atypical bridge also featured on many postcards of the time, some of which were colourized. A close inspection of the photographs reveals the names of two businesses written in vernacular signwriting: A. Scully and H. Flanagan.

The 1901 census lists the houses on the bridge and it is likely that the A. Scully was an Anne Scully, a forty-six-year-old, Offaly-born woman who lived with her three teenage children. H. Flanagan was listed in the same census as Henry Flanagin [sic.] a thirty-two-year-old married man whose occupation was given as a 'car owner and grocer'. These shopfronts included six-over-six sash windows and timber pilasters, fascias and carved cornices which were typical of the period.

Many of the houses had become derelict towards the end of the 20th century and local councillors claimed that they had become sites for antisocial behaviour. Some local conservationists expressed the opinion that they should be saved due to their age, unusual aspect and potential as a tourist attraction. The parapets were eventually replaced by metal railings and the houses were demolished in 1971. The bridge is now barely visible to passers-by.

OPPOSITE PAGE AND BELOW Two views of the bridge at Birr.

RIGHT The Leviathon of Parsonstown was an internationally famous astronomical instrument.

Ryan's Daughter was an epic film directed by David Lean. Made in 1970, it was loosely based on Gustave Flaubert's *Madame Bovary* and was filmed in County Kerry. Set against the backdrop of World War I and the struggle for Irish Independence, it tells the story of an Irish woman, Rosy Ryan, who has an affair with a shell-shocked British soldier, Major Randolph Doryan. The female lead was played by Sarah Miles, Robert Mitchum played her husband, while the soldier was played by Christopher Jones.

Lean was known for his lavish productions such as *Lawrence of Arabia* (1962) and *Doctor Zhivago* (1965) and he built an entire village, 'Kirrary', in Kerry, at the location on the Dingle Peninsula. Lean felt that it was cheaper to build a village from scratch than to deal with the random nature of a living village which would have required the eradication of modern features and control of access. The set designer was a former stage director of the Dublin Players, Josie MacAvin, who would go on to win an Academy Award for her work on *Out of Africa* (1985).

High wages were offered during the six-month construction period. Twenty film craftsmen and two hundred locals were employed to build the village of thirty houses. Eight hundred tonnes of granite were sourced from ruined cottages and hauled up the hill to the location. An abandoned railway station in Dingle was turned into a workshop for the film.

The village included a church, which was made of fibreglass; however, it did boast a working coal house and stables. Attention was paid to period detail; for example, the schoolhouse replicated the separate entrances for boys and girls. Filming took place over a twelve-month period and was often hampered by bad weather. Cinematographer Freddie Young created epic panoramic views of the Kerry scenery.

The film provided a great boost for the local economy, and in an interview, Lean revealed that he had offered the entire village to the local people upon completion of filming. He was also willing to consolidate and augment the more insubstantial buildings. But his offer was declined. Planning laws and in-fighting over the rights and ownership of the land upon which the village was located meant that it had to be demolished by the film company. Sepia-tinted postcards were made before the village was razed. The schoolhouse, which was built by a local stonemason, is the only remaining building from the set: the main Kirrary set was built on commonage land; however the schoolhouse was built on land owned by local farmers and was subsequently bought by the founder of Ryanair. After a storm in 2015, the roof fell in and it is now in a dilapidated state.

The film showed the beauty of the Kerry scenery to great effect and is credited with putting Dingle on the tourist map; however researchers have shown that tourists are disappointed that so little remains of the village. Nonetheless, Kerry continues to attract tourists and film crews. In 2015 and 2017, the monastery on Skellig Michael off the Iveragh Peninsula was used as a location for filming in Star Wars films *The Force Awakens* and *The Last Jedi*.

OPPOSITE PAGE Director David Lean talks to leading man Christopher Jones on the village set of *Ryan's Daughter*.

BELOW Robert Mitchum was cast as the school teacher Charles Shaughnessy.

BOTTOM The school building, with separate entrances for girls and boys.

ARROL GANTRY, BELFAST
DISMANTLED 1971

Shipbuilding and linen are the two industries most associated with Belfast. The best-known shipbuilding firm was Harland and Wolff and the company was responsible for the construction of the biggest White Star liners in the early 20th century.

The company was formed in 1862 by Edward James Harland and German-born Gustav Wilhelm Wolff. Their shipyard was located on reclaimed land at Queen's Island in Belfast Harbour. The Arrol Gantry was a gigantic industrial structure built in 1908 for the construction of the RMS *Olympic* and the ill-fated RMS *Titanic*, and it was to remain in use until the 1960s. The White Star Line was a British shipping company who were leaders in the provision of passenger and cargo ships to the United States of America. Almost all of their ships were built in Belfast by Harland and Wolff.

The workers at Harland and Wolff represented the greatest concentration of unionized skilled labour in Ireland. It was a highly stratified environment with twenty-two different classes of skilled trades including joiners, fitters, platers, caulkers and sawyers. Tensions existed between the skilled, semi-skilled and unskilled workers.

The peak of employment occurred during World War II when around 35,000 people worked at the shipyard. During the war, it produced 140 warships, 123 merchant ships and 500 tanks.

Shipbuilding slumped in the post-war period as air travel dominated transatlantic journeys, and cheap labour in other shipbuilding countries left Northern Ireland at an economic disadvantage. Harland and Wolff began to take down the Arrol Gantry in 1971. The process took several years and it was taken away for scrap metal. It was replaced by two cranes, known as Samson and Delilah, which are now monumental features on the Belfast skyline. While not on a preservation list, they are given special recognition by preservation bodies and are considered to be of historical interest.

Harland and Wolff was nationalized by the Labour government in 1977 and then privatized in 1989. In the latter years the company diversified into work such as the maintenance of oil rigs. It ceased trading and entered formal administration in August 2019. Although

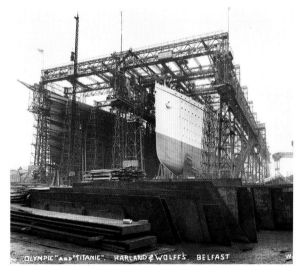

a buyer was found for the business, it provided work for just seventy-nine employees. Meanwhile, the area around the shipyard has undergone regeneration in recent years with the opening of the Titanic Museum, and the former drawing offices are now a boutique hotel.

OPPOSITE PAGE Photographed in the 1950s, the Arrol Gantry was built by Sir William Arrol & Co.

TOP The *Titanic* slips quietly into the waters of the River Lagan.

ABOVE LEFT The *Titanic* and *Olympic* under construction circa 1909. The *Olympic* (right) was launched in 1910.

ABOVE Workers stream away from the Harland and Wolff shipyard on Queen's Island circa 1911.

DUBLIN CATTLE MARKET
CLOSED 1973

The Dublin Cattle Market was located on the North Circular Road between Prussia Street and Aughrim Street. This bustling area of the city came to be known as 'Cowtown'. At one time it was the largest weekly livestock sale in Europe.

The market was established by the Dublin Corporation in 1863 to replace an existing, more ad hoc, market at Smithfield. The move sought to improve sanitary conditions and offer a more convenient location for sellers and buyers. Work on the site commenced in February 1863 and the market was formally opened on the 24th of November 1863. From 1867, running water was piped to the market via the new Vartry Reservoir in County Wicklow which allowed for a more thorough cleaning of the open-air, metal-railed pens.

The market set the prices for cattle fairs throughout the country. Cattle came mainly from the counties of Meath, Dublin, Kildare, Westmeath and Offaly. Prior to the sales, the cattle were often kept in cattle parks in nearby suburbs such as Castleknock and had to be driven through the streets to the market. In later years most were transported by rail. The market had pens to process around 5,000 head of cattle.

The busiest times of the year were between August and November, when grass-fed cattle were sold. The British buyers arrived the evening before the sales and there were many attendant businesses such as hotels and public houses to cater to their needs. There were as many as eleven public houses located in the two streets nearest to the market. The gates opened for livestock at 3 a.m. and the sales started at 5 a.m.

The market's business peaked in the 1950s. It is estimated that nearly three quarters of a million animals went through the market per annum and the bulk of the live sales went to Britain. After the market, cattle were driven along the streets of Dublin to either abattoirs or to the docks at the North Wall where they were exported live to Britain or continental Europe.

The Cattle Market is referenced several times in James Joyce's *Ulysses* as the main character, Bloom, once worked for the cattle dealer Joseph Cuffe. Bloom and his wife also lived in the City Arms Hotel which was attached to the market. This had once

been the home of the Jameson family upon whose land the market was built. The second lessee was Moses Dowd, whose daughter, Elizabeth O'Dowd, ran the Cattle Market Hotel, later the City Arms Hotel, for many decades. Branches of international banks had desks in the foyer of the City Arms Hotel in order to facilitate the large transactions that were undertaken.

Several outbreaks of foot-and-mouth disease, the rise of local marts, factory abattoirs, and the sheer inconvenience of a city location reduced the business of the market. The last sale took place in May 1973. Social housing was constructed on the site between 1978 and 1980.

OPPOSITE PAGE At one time Dublin Cattle Market ran the biggest weekly livestock sale in Europe.

ABOVE Cattle are driven through the streets to the market. In his novel *Ulysses*, James Joyce elaborates in great detail about Bloom's plan to run a tram to the docks which would transport the cattle there.

CATTLE MARKET. DUBLIN. 89/0. W.L.

HOTEL METROPOLE. SACKVILLE St. DUBLIN. 4818. W. L.

METROPOLE HOTEL / METROPOLE CINEMA, DUBLIN

DEMOLISHED 1916/1973

The grand Metropole Hotel was located next to the General Post Office on Dublin's main thoroughfare, Sackville Street (subsequently O'Connell Street). William Mansfield Mitchell was the architect who unified four Georgian buildings in his plans, executed between 1891 and 1893. His design included ornate ironwork verandas on the first three floors of the hotel. This location was at the centre of the fighting during the Easter Rising in 1916 and the hotel was at one stage occupied by the rebels using its kitchens to prepare food for the other garrisons. It was completely destroyed in the fighting.

The replacement building was an entertainment complex including a cinema, restaurant, ballroom and a bar. It was neoclassical in design and the work of the architect Aubrey V. O'Rourke. He specialized in cinemas and hotels and his work included the Pillar Picture House and Mary Street Picture House. He also designed the Four Courts Hotel, Moran's Hotel and Michael Guiney's store on Talbot Street. He appears to have undertaken a considerable amount of reconstruction work following the destruction of the 1916 Rising and the Civil War. His brother Horace was the city architect responsible for planning in the post-Rising period. The renowned architect who designed some of the more innovative social housing schemes in Dublin, George Herbert Simms, was one of his assistants.

The new five-storey Metropole opened in 1922 with a film starring the child actor Jackie Coogan. At one stage the complex employed two hundred people and at the heart of the enterprise was a 1,000-seater cinema. The interior included classical Corinthian columns and a dome decorated with scenes from Shakespeare's plays.

The Metropole was at the centre of the city's social and cultural life. In 1927, a new canopy was added over the restaurant entrance on Princes Street. The Metropole's restaurant was called the Georgian Rooms, and advertisements from the 1960s state that it offered dinner, cabaret and dancing from 6 p.m.

Cinema-going in Ireland was at its pinnacle in 1954 with more than fifty-four million admissions in that year alone. In tandem with the growth in television ownership the numbers going to the cinema decreased from the 1960s onwards.

The owners of the Metropole, the Rank Organisation, cut their losses and sold the building in 1972. It was demolished in 1973 along with the Capitol Cinema on North Princes Street. A new British Home Stores shop was the street-level occupant of the building that replaced it.

OPPOSITE PAGE While the General Post Office facade (next door) remained intact after the 1916 fighting, the Metropole was completely destroyed.

BELOW The movie *Valdez is Coming*, starring Burt Lancaster, dates this photo of the Metropole Cinema to 1971. Occupying a prime position next to the GPO it was always likely to be a target for redevelopment.

ST. CONLETH'S BOYS REFORMATORY, DAINGEAN, OFFALY

CLOSED 1973

The town of Daingean is in the midlands county of Offaly. It was previously known as Philipstown after King Philip II of Spain. He had married the Catholic English Queen Mary during the 16th-century plantation (or colonization) of Ireland and held the titles King of Spain, King of Portugal and, briefly (from 1554 to 1558), the King of England and King of Ireland. During this period the county of Offaly was known as King's County. As the main county town, Daingean had impressive buildings such as the James Gandon-designed courthouse. Other notable buildings were the Old Foot Barracks and the Old Gaol from where prisoners were transported to Australia in the mid 19th century.

The town is surrounded by the Bog of Allen, and the Grand Canal also runs through it, as is visible in the aerial photograph below. This canal connects Dublin city to the River Shannon and was constructed during a massive engineering project between 1756 and 1804. It took more than five years for the builders of the canal to traverse the Bog of Allen and it reached Philipstown in 1797. For a period the canal terminated in the town, which was economically beneficial; however, when it was extended to the town of Tullamore, the attendant business left with it. In 1837, Samuel Lewis, in his *Topographical Dictionary of Ireland*, wrote, 'The town has little to recommend it; being nearly surrounded by bog, it is extremely uninteresting.' The transfer of county town status to Tullamore in the 1880s was also detrimental to Daingean's economy and status.

Daingean is perhaps best known, however, for the infamous Boys Reformatory in which boys who were convicted of crimes between the ages of twelve and seventeen, were committed for between two and four years. The Oblates of Mary Immaculate, a religious order, ran the reformatory at Daingean from 1870 until 1973. The original buildings had been constructed as a military barracks in the middle of the 18th century. Before becoming a reformatory it had also been used as a training academy for the Irish Constabulary and was briefly an adult prison.

The complex was surrounded by massive stone walls and it included dormitories, a piggery, a poultry house, scullery, storerooms and church. Sixty-seven acres (27 hectares) of adjacent land were rented. The boys who were sent to St. Conleth's tended to be from the urban working classes and their detention ceased at the age of nineteen. *The Report of the Commission to Inquire into Child Abuse* (2009), also known as *The Ryan Report*, detailed the shocking abuses that children endured there. The report stated that the Department of Education displayed 'ambivalence to the use of violence in Daingean, even as late as 1969', while Brother Enrico was responsible for 'severe ad hoc punishments' and 'the more ritualistic floggings'.

This aerial photograph is part of the Morgan collection which was taken by Captain Alexander Campbell Morgan in the 1950s. These low-altitude photos were published in the *Irish Independent* newspaper as part of a column entitled 'Ireland from the Air'. In this unique view of the reformatory, it is possible to see how fully enclosed the complex was, with little hope of escape. It is a rare glimpse into the reformatory grounds during its operation.

Part of the site is now used to house the Folk Life Collection of the National Museum of Ireland, while other buildings have fallen into disrepair. The future of the complex, which houses a wide variety of buildings and which tells an important story for modern Ireland, remains uncertain.

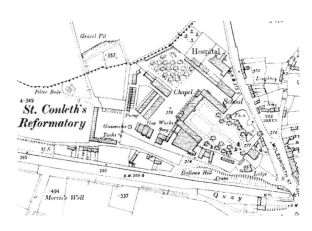

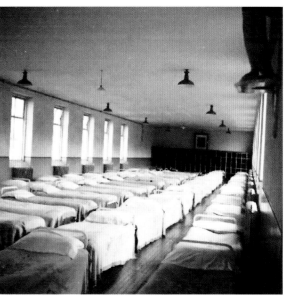

OPPOSITE PAGE Captain Morgan's aerial photo from the 1950s shows that the hospital building documented on the early 1900s Ordnance Survey map (top) had been demolished. Captain Morgan was killed in an air accident in 1958.

ABOVE One of the boys' dormitories.

LEFT The Grand Canal is clearly visible below the Reformatory walls.

FRENCH-STYLE URINALS, DUBLIN
LAST ONE SCRAPPED 1980

In preparation for the 1932 Eucharistic Congress, Dublin City Corporation imported and installed outdoor French-style urinals often known as 'pissoirs'. The Congress was an international event celebrating the Roman Catholic Sacrament of the Eucharist. The Dublin congregation was one of the largest ever with over a million people attending the final Mass at the end of the week-long spectacle. The new public toilets, however, were to meet the needs of the male pilgrims only and no extra female toilets were installed. They were mainly located along the quays on the route towards Phoenix Park where the main events took place.

Also known as *vespasiennes*, they were devised as a solution to the problem of public urination in Paris. At the height of their popularity in the French capital there were over 1,400 of them. The models installed in Ireland were completely enclosed and octagonal in form, somewhat akin to the shape of a pepper mill. They were topped with ornate ironwork and painted dark green, and their exterior panels were used for advertising, as per this example taken by Elinor Wiltshire. Several recent autobiographies have cited them as a location for homosexual cruising and casual sex in Dublin city centre .

As drug use increased in the city in the late 1970s, public toilets came to be viewed as locations that facilitated antisocial behaviour. The last of the 1932 pissoirs in Dublin city was located in the northern suburb of Fairview, at the junction of the Malahide Road, until it was removed in 1980. It was also purported that one of the final pissoirs was sold to a student for £10 and that it ended up being used as a garden gazebo in Sandymount (minus the porcelain).

Many bemoan the loss of Dublin's rich variety of street furniture, which included the railings, streetlamps, bollards and kerbstones that gave the city a unique look and added to the streetscape. In recent years all of Dublin's public toilets have been removed.

Indeed, during the economic boom of the Celtic Tiger the sites were often sold off to developers. This has provoked discussions as to the privatization of public space and the council's obligations to its citizens.

These arguments, and the lack of public toilets for women, are echoed in Irish fictional works, most notably in Flann O'Brien's comic novel *The Hard Life* (1961) in which a character called Mr Collopy mounts a lifelong campaign to force the Dublin Corporation to provide public toilets for women.

The lack of female public toilets is also mentioned briefly in James Joyce's *Ulysses* (1922) when the novel's main character, Leopold Bloom, walks by the male urinals near to a statue of the poet Thomas Moore and observes that there should also be toilets for women.

OPPOSITE PAGE AND LEFT A little touch of Paris is now believed to reside in a garden in Sandymount. Coincidentally, one of Ireland's greatest actors, Cyril Cusack, played the mayor of the fictional town of Clochemerle in France. The BBC television series *Clochemerle* was a comedy drama about the siting of a similar 'pissoir' in the town and the furore it provoked.

LADIES BATHS / MOORISH BATHS
BRAY, COUNTY WICKLOW
CLOSED 1965 / DEMOLISHED 1980

The Moorish Baths at Bray were opened in the County Wicklow seaside town in 1859 by the Earl of Meath. The railway had expanded to reach the town five years earlier and Bray had soon become a bustling and busy tourist attraction for both day-trippers and holidaymakers. Seaside resorts had a reputation for restoring health through exposure to fresh air and to spa treatments such as hydrotherapy. The water cure was purported to solve a variety of ailments from alcoholism to tuberculosis.

The Moorish Baths in Bray was one of several established in Ireland by Dr. Richard Barter in which he applied his 'improved' system of bathing. He called them Roman-Irish baths and considered them to be an improvement on the traditional Turkish hammam. His treatment involved the application of dry heat (as opposed to wet heat) during which the bather progressed through a number of increasingly hotter rooms interspersed with several plunges into cold water. Dr. Barter had branches in Cork city, Belfast, Limerick and Killarney, and his largest was a full institution called St. Ann's Hydropathic Establishment, in Blarney, County Cork.

The engineer and railway advocate William Dargan supported the Baths financially to the tune of £10,000. He had been instrumental in getting the railway line extended to Bray and he invested heavily in the town, transforming it from a poor fishing village into a vibrant resort. The Baths' architect was Sir John Benson, who had worked with Dargan on the design of the main pavilions at the Great Industrial Exhibition of 1853 which Dargan had funded. He was also involved in the design of railway stations and Dr. Barter's baths at Lincoln Place in Dublin city centre (as visited by Leopold Bloom in *Ulysses*).

An official guidebook to the locality published in the 1860s provides a detailed account of the building. The facade was described as red and white in colour with many minarets and a flight of stone steps. The interior was lavish and decorated in arabesque designs with marble seats and stained glass. Other features included a large mirrored octagonal pillar, heated

floors and couches upon which customers could recline and sip cold water. Bathers wore wooden clogs and loose, sheet-like garments. The enterprise was not successful. By the winter of 1862 customers were being offered free entry, and despite a price tag of £4000, Dargan failed to sell the building in 1864. In 1867 the building was converted into assembly rooms for concerts and other functions. After having its ornate brick frontage rendered around 1900 it was converted into a cinema and subsequently became derelict, lingering on until demolition in 1980.

Far more popular, but not as long-lasting was the Ladies Baths between Strand Road and the esplanade. These Victorian baths were fiercely opposed by some

residents of Strand Road who realised their direct view to the seafront was going to be obscured. Nevertheless it was opened in 1879 and lasted through till 1965 when it was demolished and replaced by public toilets and an aquarium.

OPPOSITE PAGE The Ladies Baths on the seafront at Bray.

ABOVE Dr. Barter's Moorish Baths in Bray were a spectacular business failure, but a tremendous example of Irish craftsmen replicating Ottoman architecture.

MARINE STATION HOTEL. BRAY.

MARINE STATION HOTEL, INTERNATIONAL HOTEL, BRAY, COUNTY WICKLOW

REPURPOSED 1936/DEMOLISHED 1980

The twelve-room Marine Hotel was opened by Edward Breslin in 1855. Breslin had provided the catering for the Great Industrial Exhibition of 1853 and was an associate of William Dargan who was keen to open up Bray as a tourist destination after the railway he promoted arrived in 1854. Along with landowner John Quin and builder John Brennan – a Bray man who had made his fortune in America – they set about making Bray the Brighton of Ireland.

Business was good at first and Breslin expanded the Marine in 1859, about the same time as the Dargan-funded Moorish Baths were being opened. By 1870 his hotel had been renamed the Royal Marine Hotel and subsequently the Marine Station Hotel to emphasize its proximity to Bray Station.

Compared to the Marine, the International Hotel was a comparative latecomer to the tourist trade in Bray, first opening its doors in 1862. Dargan had obtained a 900-year lease of a prime site from John Quin for £50 a year, and the lease obliged him to build a house or hotel fronting onto Quinsborough Road. Strategically positioned opposite the railway station, the hotel that John Brennan built for £30,000 was named after the International Exhibition in London. It could easily have been called the Grand Hotel.

OPPOSITE PAGE The Marine Station Hotel was still thriving at the turn of the century.

BELOW The original Breslin's Marine Hotel with its entrance facing Quinsborough Road.

BRESLIN'S MARINE HOTEL. BRAY.
Situate on the Beach & immediately contiguous to the Railway Station.

It was the largest hotel in Ireland at the time, boasting 212 bedrooms, and its stated aim was to 'provide a continental hotel experience'.

But it may have been too large. Dargan's Moorish Baths was losing money by 1862 and he soon had to sell the International which had three changes of ownership in the 1860s alone.

The Marine Hotel changed hands in 1909, selling to the Dublin, Wicklow & Wexford Railway Co. who operated the Hotel up until World War I. A fire badly damaged the upper floors of the hotel in 1916 and it lay dormant through the years of civil unrest and the Great Depression, until 1935.

The Great War had a profound effect on the economy of the town, reliant as it was on the tourist trade. Hospitals and sanitariums throughout the British Isles were filled to capacity and so large hotels were commandeered. The British Red Cross and the St. John Ambulance Association leased the International from owner Frank Bethell from 1915, renaming it The Princess Patricia Hospital for Wounded Soldiers. The two hundred-bed hospital was initially used for convalescing soldiers discharged from the Dublin hospitals, but as the war went on, more severely wounded men were treated there.

The International was returned to Frank Bethell in 1919 but the hotel was not reopened. In 1921 the furnishings were sold off by auction and it stood vacant and neglected from 1922 to 1935. Together with the semi-derelict Marine Hotel on the corner of Strand and Quinsborough Roads the two hotels made a pretty poor sight to anyone arriving at Bray Station.

In the mid 1930s this all changed. For a short while, from 1934, the A. P. Friendship Holidays Association of London, took over and ran the International Hotel. The lower floors of the Marine Hotel that had survived the fire were reopened in 1936 as the Railway Buffet. The hotel was eventually sold in the 1960s and the lower floors rebuilt in 1998. Today the building facing the Irish Sea on the corner of Quinsborough Road and Strand Road closely follows the footprint of the old Marine Hotel and is now the Ocean Bar and Grill.

During World War II, Bray became a garrison town for the Irish army with the Fifth Battalion based in the International Hotel. It re-opened for visitors in 1947, but like so many times before, it struggled for business. It was put up for sale by auction in 1950 but failed to meet reserve. It was eventually sold in 1961 and the new owners followed the path of so many previous

operators; it was refurbished, re-opened and closed a few years later, coming back onto the market in 1964.

It struggled on in business until 1974, when a fire on June 14th took hold and destroyed the grand building. What remained of the shell was deemed unsafe by the council and so the site was cleared. After a 16-year wait, Bray Leisure Bowl was constructed on the site in 1990.

OPPOSITE PAGE AND ABOVE Further up Quinsborough Road the International Hotel was built in a more elaborate, embellished style than the Marine and with a far greater occupancy. However it lacked the Marine's sea views.

INTERNATIONAL HOTEL. BRAY. 457. W.L.

PORTLAW COTTON FACTORY, COUNTY WATERFORD

CLOSED 1985

The gigantic cotton factory complex at Portlaw, County Waterford, was built by the Malcolmson family in the 1820s. It included a canal which transported raw materials from America (via Liverpool) directly to their factory. The finished goods were then taken to Waterford port and exported across the world. When the operation started, there were 395 people living in the village of Portlaw and by its peak in the 1850s the factory employed 1,862 workers. The factory was in operation for twenty-four hours a day and it employed a high number of female workers whose tasks included spinning, carding and reeling cotton.

This Quaker family had a paternalistic attitude towards their workers, building a model village for them. The industrial village included a central square, from which radiated five streets, and included a temperance hall and a thrift society. John Skipton Mulvany, who was also the architect for Broadstone Station in Dublin, had a hand in the design of the employee homes, which were an unusual design for Ireland as they had semi-flat roofs and 12-foot-high (3.7-metre) interior ceilings. The Malcolmsons built single and two-storey houses for their employees and each had a private yard and large vegetable plot. They also built a school, and even though children worked part-time, they had to attend school in order to get their wages. The village had its own currency in the form of tokens known as 'leather money', which were valid within a 30-mile radius. These were in circulation until 1876.

The American Civil War (1861–1865) precipitated the downfall of the factory as exports of raw materials from the Southern states were curtailed. The factory's continued reliance on canals for transportation also caused difficulties; the arrival of the railways meant that other companies were able to move their goods more quickly. Following these downturns, mill workers emigrated to England, Scotland and America with many going to the Fall River, Massachusetts – a town which had more than a hundred cotton mills and where many of the workers were Irish immigrants.

The cotton mill in Portlaw closed in 1876, with the Mayfield Spinning Company ceasing production in

1904. A large portion of the factory was then converted into the Mayfield Dairy Company. In 1932, the site was taken over by the Irish Tanners Ltd. This endeavour was part of the Irish government's protectionist policies which sought to support indigenous industries and supplant imports. A new tannery and extensions were added in the 1940s; however, cheap plastic imports resulted in a decline in demand for leather-soled shoes of the type made in Portlaw. The factory finally closed in 1985 and is now in a ruinous state.

OPPOSITE PAGE The Malcolmson family built several impressive homes in the vicinity of the factory including the Italianate Mayfield House (right), which is now derelict. The National Trust for Ireland, An Taisce, fear that it could collapse at any time.

BELOW The magnificent mill building photographed from the campanile tower of Mayfield House.

IRISH HOSPITALS SWEEPSTAKES OFFICES, BALLSBRIDGE

CLOSED 1987

A sleek office complex was built between 1937 and 1938 to house the operations of the Irish Hospitals Sweepstakes. The stakes were set up in 1930 in order to fund the construction of hospitals in the new Irish state. Tickets were sold in over 180 countries and the majority were purchased outside of Ireland. Each ticket was assigned a horse in the large races held in England and Ireland and everyone who entered received a handwritten receipt. Over the course of its history it paid out millions in prize money and put the proceeds towards hospital building programmes. The sweepstakes were ostensibly a charity, although recent research has shown that not all the money made it into the government exchequer and that the individuals running the trust were paid substantial wages and dividends.

When the previous building burnt down in 1935, the architectural firm of Robinson & Keefe were hired to build a new headquarters in the South Dublin location of Donnybrook. John Joseph Robinson and Richard Cyril Keefe were well known for their cinemas, factories and technical schools. Robinson had also been the official architect to the Eucharistic Congress which took place in Dublin in 1932. The building was set on eleven acres and it had modern features like porthole windows, glass bricks and teak and terrazzo flooring throughout. Photographs show vast open-plan spaces with thousands of employees at work in offices that were quite industrial in their design. At its peak the Irish Sweepstakes employed 4,000 clerical workers, most of whom were women.

The draws were big events given to much pomp and pageant, with some of the elaborate sets attaining Hollywood-like levels of production. Attractive young nurses featured widely in the promotional material and the tickets themselves were lavish designs using the latest typography and printing techniques. The company mascot was called Big Tom, a cartoon black cat who was displayed at outlets. The Sweepstakes also organized parades through the streets of Dublin before every draw, with all the tickets carried in boxes accompanied by a huge *papier mâché* lucky elephant.

Sales declined in the 1970s and 1980s. The company did not win the contract to run the new national state lottery and it closed in 1987. There was much acrimony among the staff, many of whom were women over fifty who were in the long-term employ of the stakes and did not have pension entitlements, and also for whom inadequate social insurance rates had been paid over the years. The headquarters were demolished and another office development was built in its place in 1991.

OPPOSITE PAGE Using engineer F. F. Warren's giant revolving drum, nurses pull the winning tickets in March 1964.

BELOW LEFT The Lucky Elephant makes its way down Middle Abbey Street in the 1935 pre-Sweepstake parade.

BELOW The vast administrative office at Ballsbridge.

ASPRO FACTORY, DUBLIN
DEMOLISHED 1987

One of the finest examples of early modern architecture in Ireland, the Aspro factory in Inchicore, Dublin, was built between 1947 and 1949. Aspro was a variant of the drug aspirin. The factory's construction pre-dates the Irish government's progressive post-war economic policies of the 1950s, which fostered the gradual move away from over-dependence upon agriculture and a protectionism of indigenous industries. Nonetheless, its construction signalled an emergence from the doldrums of the 1930s and a push towards manufacturing.

The building's architect was Liverpool-born Alan Hope, who had moved to Ireland in the early 1930s. Constructed by one of Ireland's largest building firms, G. & T. Crampton, the bright, open Aspro factory exemplified an International style of modernism with its white rendered curves, extensive glazing and flat roof. Rex Robertson's crisp black and white photographs show the distinctive spiral staircase which was the centrepiece of the building.

The building was divided into three zones: industrial, recreational and administrative. The complex also included an area where health screening and medical care could take place. This and the inclusion of a staff canteen indicates the progressive type of employer that the country wished to attract. Set back from the road in landscaped grounds, the factory was clearly visible to cars travelling along the Naas Road.

It is thought that the inspiration for the factory's design and layout came from the beautiful Art Deco De La Warr Pavilion at Bexhill-on-Sea in East Sussex, England. The factory was formally opened by the Minister for Industry and Commerce, Daniel Morrissey, on the 1st of June 1949. He welcomed the progressive social conditions that the factory offered its employees and also lauded the replacement of imports with domestically produced goods. The factory remained profitable throughout the 1950s and 1960s.

Alan Hope was awarded the Triennial Gold Medal by the Royal Institute of Architects of Ireland (R.I.A.I.) in 1950 for the Aspro Factory. Despite this accolade, 20th-century modernism was little appreciated by subsequent generations. The building was sold in the late 1960s and was used for a period as a car showroom. The award-winning factory was one of the few 20th-century buildings that were listed as worthy of preservation by the Dublin Corporation. Nonetheless, it was hurriedly demolished over a weekend in July 1987. Letters of protest were sent to various national newspapers but no reparation or attempts to reinstate the building were subsequently made.

OPPOSITE PAGE AND ABOVE Such was the quality of the design of the Aspro Factory that it won its architect, Alan Hope, the RIAI Triennial Gold Medal, awarded every three years. Other winning buildings have included Cork Institute of Technology Library and Croke Park.

YORK STREET SPINNING MILL, BELFAST

DEMOLISHED 1988

The York Street Spinning Mill in Belfast was founded by Alexander Mulholland in 1830. The firm was to become the largest flax spinners, linen manufacturers and distributors in the world and at one point it employed four thousand workers. Linen from Belfast came to dominate the British and American markets. Products included high-quality damask tablecloths, napkins and handkerchiefs, along with dress linen. Mulholland converted the factory from cotton to flax, taking advantage of the lack of cotton caused by the American Civil War. He was also quick to mechanize and modernize. The linen industry was fully mechanized by

the 1860s, with power looms increasing the capacity of the Belfast factories. Mulholland's factory was five storeys high and its architect was Jackson Thomas. The complex also featured a 186-foot (57-metre) chimney. By the 1910s, linen and shipbuilding were the two main industries in the city, and Belfast became so synonymous with the linen industry that it gained the nickname 'Linenopolis'. Among the other large mills in the city were Jennymount in North Belfast and Greeve's Mill in the West.

About half of the employees were women or girls, who worked long hours in noisy, sometimes

BELOW At one time Belfast was the world leader in linen production and the York Street Mill was the largest exporter.

White Lapping Room York St. Factory Belfast.

R.W. 1242.

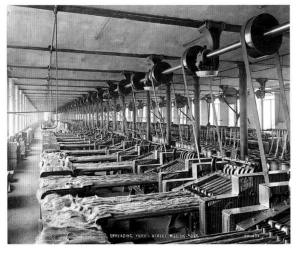

Spreading York Street Mill Belfast.

White Ornamenting Room York Street Mill Belfast.

dangerous, conditions. Spinning and weaving were undertaken in conditions of high humidity, and fibrous dust caused respiratory diseases. In 1874, the starting age for children in the mill was ten years old, though this had risen to twelve by 1901. Children worked on the half-time system which meant that they went to school on alternate days. Long working hours were the norm, with most working from 6.30 a.m. to 6 p.m. Wages were not high and it is thought that this is what helped Belfast maintain its competitiveness on the global market. The 1911 census recorded 30,000 people engaged in linen production in Belfast alone. Four thousand of these were employed in the York Street Mill. Work was divided along sectarian lines: the majority of the lower-paid, lower-skilled female mill workers were Catholic while the higher-paid weavers were Protestant.

During World War II, the York Street Mill was involved in military production and manufactured linen for covering aircraft and glider frames. In the Belfast Blitz of April and May 1941, the factory was bombed by the German Luftwaffe, taking a direct hit on the 15th of April. One of the enormous walls fell down onto workers' houses on Sussex and Vere streets, killing thirty-five residents. A new spinning mill was built in 1953 to designs by Samuel Stevenson & Sons, but in the post-war period the rise of cheap, synthetic materials took over and one-third of Northern Ireland's spinning mills had closed by 1964.

The York Street Spinning Mill closed in 1961 and it then became a Gallaher's tobacco factory, which in turn shut its doors in 1988. A shopping centre is now located on the site. Many of the other mills have also fallen into ruin, though Conway Mills is now run by a preservation trust and is used as an exhibition and community space.

OPPOSITE PAGE Warping machinery at work. Warping is the process of combining yarns from different cones.

TOP LEFT The White Lapping room where sheets of linen were cut and folded.

FAR LEFT The Spreading Room.

LEFT The White Ornamenting room. The National Museums of Northern Ireland archive has many more detailed photos of the York Street Spinning Mill that illustrate all the processes involved in producing linen there.

PHOENIX PARK RACECOURSE, DUBLIN
CLOSED 1990

Ireland has an international reputation for horse breeding and racing, and for over ninety years, the Phoenix Park Racecourse played an important part in the racing calendar. Located on the northern edge of Phoenix Park, one of the largest enclosed parks in Europe, the course was founded by Cork-born J. H. H. Peard, and racing began there in 1902.

The first races took place at the end of Horse Show week in August of that year. Peard, who was a qualified veterinary surgeon, oversaw the course layout and fixtures. His partners included Sir John Arnott and Major Eustace Loder. William Charles Manning of Newry, County Down, designed the racecourse. He had previously worked as the architect and surveyor at the famous Newmarket Jockey Club in England. The landscape architect Thomas Smith was responsible for the planting, with shrubs sourced from his Daisy Hill nursery. He was also responsible

for the garden at the Irish Pavilion at the Glasgow International Exhibition in 1901.

The architect Edwin Bradbury, who designed Ashtown Lodge, the half-timbered Tudor revival home of the Arnott family in 1909, may also have been responsible for the design of the racecourse buildings, which are in a similar style. During their 1903 visit, the royal couple Edward VII and Queen Alexandra visited a race meeting at Phoenix Park.

The complex included several grandstands, pavilions, gate lodges, ticket kiosks and turnstiles in a Tudor revival style. It was considered a fashionable meeting and was reported to have a garden party atmosphere with brass bands playing in a bandstand. Evening races were a particularly popular attraction.

The Midland Great Western Railway decided to build a new train station at Ashtown in order to accommodate racegoers.

In the years after World War II, the racecourse attracted visitors from Britain, and the society pages and magazines were full of photographs of lords and ladies attending the various meetings. A Bollinger Champagne bar was opened in the early 1970s.

In the 1980s the racecourse hosted several large rock concerts, with U2 playing there in 1983. During this period the complex also included a nightclub called Silks. The course staged the richest two-year-old race in the world, the Phoenix Plate, with prize money of half a million punts and yearly attendances of 95,000. Peard's descendants ran the course until the 1980s after which it closed for a period. A group of businessmen attempted to revive the racecourse; however it eventually closed for good in September 1990. The racecourse grandstand and Ashtown Lodge were damaged by fire in 1998 and the site was partially developed for housing. An apartment complex now occupies half of the site as the economic downturn halted further development. None of the original buildings remain.

OPPOSITE PAGE An aerial photo of the grandstands and paddocks from the late 1950s.

LEFT Horses are paraded before the Cartier Million race in the 1980s.

BELOW The parade ring with completed central grandstand in 1987.

GATE LODGES, PORTLAW AND SUMMERHILL
DEMOLISHED 1990s

It has been estimated that Ireland once had 10,000 gate lodges. The majority were built in the 18th and 19th centuries, and they were positioned at the entrance to grand estates. They were occupied by the gate porter, a kind of live-in security guard, who opened and closed the gates to the demesne and generally kept an eye on the comings and goings around the property. They usually preceded tree-lined drives, and larger estates had multiple lodges and entrances. The porter or lodge keeper was one of the many staff employed on a landed estate during a period when wages were low.

With the break-up of the large estates and their 'Big Houses', at least forty per cent of the gate lodges have gone. These diminutive buildings were built in a wide variety of architectural styles and they often offered the landlord an opportunity to experiment with whimsical or novel designs. Some were designed from templates which could be found in books such as the British architect Peter Frederick Robinson's 1833 publication *Designs for Gate Cottages, Lodges and Park Entrances*. Visible from the road to the passer-by and visitor alike they were an important indicator of the estate's character and standing. They were both ornamental and functional.

The unusual gate lodge in the main image once stood in the grounds of Milford House in County Waterford, home of the Malcolmson family, the owners of the Portlaw Cotton factory. The ornate ironwork veranda wrapped around the circular copper-roofed building. The densely patterned ironwork included fan-shaped palm leaves at regular intervals, supposedly referencing a Swiss chalet.

Some photographs show that greenery was trained around the veranda. It had a basement and the fireplaces were placed into a central pillar. Milford House was one of several houses built by the Malcolmson family in the area. John Skipton Mulvany, who is best known for Broadstone Train Station in Dublin and the Dún Laoghaire and Galway railway stations, was the family's favourite architect.

Their wealth was based on copper and cotton and they built the nearby model village of Portlaw for their workers. The main house was destroyed by fire and the site is now the Woodlands housing estate. The massive gates visible in this picture were sold and are now located at the Woodhouse Estate in Stradbally, County Laois. Milford House was demolished in the mid 20th century, although a mural depicting the Copper House was painted in the village of Portlaw in 2018.

The gate lodge known as the Balloon House located at Drumlargan, County Meath, guarded the estate of Lord Langford. He was the owner of Summerhill House, a massive house with over a hundred bedrooms. It was designed by Edward Lovett Pearce and completed by Richard Cassels in the Palladian style. The Balloon House was one of a pair of similar gate lodges built in the 1850s. The main house was completely destroyed in the Civil War when it was set on fire by the Irish Republican Army on the 4th of February 1921. The ruin was totally demolished in 1970. The Balloon Houses were photographed by the architectural historian Maurice Craig in the 1970s; however, both have since been demolished.

OPPOSITE PAGE The unique Copper Lodge at Milford House.

BELOW The Balloon House at Summerhill.

PORTLAW HOUSE. 4064. W.L.

RITZ CINEMA, BELFAST

DEMOLISHED 1993

Located at the corner of Fisherwick Place and Grosvenor Road in Belfast's city centre, the Ritz was the largest cinema in Northern Ireland. Occupying an entire block, this Art Deco 2,200-seater had a central location and epitomized the glamour of 1930s cinema-going.

Built by the Union Cinema Company in 1936, its architects were Kemp & Tasker, an English firm who specialized in cinema design. Much of the building's capacity was taken up by a gigantic balcony supported by a girder manufactured at the shipbuilders Harland and Wolff. The complex also included a maple-floored ballroom and a silver-service restaurant called the Rotunda. At its peak it employed sixty uniformed staff, with the managers wearing tuxedos. The exterior of the building was highlighted with the name of the cinema emblazoned seven times in neon on its facade. Its location was prone to flooding and the cinema was closed on several occasions due to water damage. Local lore also purports that the cinema was haunted by the ghosts of a man and woman who were killed on the site, once the location of a fair.

The cinema housed a magnificent Compton theatre organ, the distinctive type of pipe organ originally developed to provide music and sound effects to accompany silent films. These organs had built-in lighting and were encased and surrounded in elaborate decorative pillars. Rising dramatically from the orchestra pit, they were used for sing-alongs long after talkies had been introduced.

The Ritz Cinema was opened by Gracie Fields, the English actress and comedian who was, in 1936, at the height of her fame. The programme opened with *Queen of Hearts*, a musical drama starring Fields alongside John Loder.

Box-office hits at the Ritz included the Cliff Richard musical *The Young Ones* (1961), which broke records on the Saturday of its first screening. Famous performers included the Beatles, who played at the Ritz in 1963. Such was the crowd of teenagers that three hundred policemen were required to stop eager fans from crushing the band. The Rolling Stones would also play two shows at the Ritz in 1965, as well as Bob Dylan in 1966.

As in other locations, cinema attendance in Northern Ireland declined with the increase in TV ownership. The Troubles were also a death knell for many cinemas, as curfews and fear of violence made the city centre a no-go area after dark. In 1977, after it had been renamed the ABC Cinema, several incendiary devices hidden in seats were activated, resulting in a fire that completely gutted the cinema auditorium and collapsed the roof. The ABC reopened four years later with four smaller screens. The cinema was eventually demolished in 1994 and is now the site of a hotel.

OPPOSITE PAGE The Ritz at the time of opening in 1936 with posters advertising Gracie Fields' latest film.

BELOW Excited crowds gather outside the Ritz in November 1963 awaiting the arrival of the Beatles.

PORTNOO HOTEL, NARIN, DONEGAL

DEMOLISHED 1994

The Portnoo Hotel, near the small coastal village of Narin, was opened by Cormac (also known as Connie) Cannon in 1890. At first it was called The Temperance Hotel. Hotels, which refrained from serving alcoholic beverages, retained their popularity into the early 20th century. The peak in the Catholic abstinence movement had occurred in the mid 19th century with the work of Father Theobald Mathew; nonetheless, the founding of the Pioneer Total Abstinence Association of the Sacred Heart by James Cullen in 1898 may have prolonged the need for such establishments. Cannon also owned another temperance hotel in the nearby town of Glenties.

In addition to the hospitality trade, Cannon was involved in the local spinning and weaving industry and he exhibited his Donegal homespun materials at the World's Fair in St. Louis in 1904. When the British Conservative politician Arthur Balfour undertook his tour of Donegal in 1890, Cannon's tweed factory was one of his destinations.

Portnoo was a seaside resort located a few miles from the railway terminus at Glenties. The hotel included a roof garden which allowed visitors to take the air and admire the scenic view. Narin Strand is a 1.2-mile (2-kilometre) sandy beach, and safe bathing was one of the attractions highlighted in notices advertising the hotel. The front of the building faced over the Atlantic Ocean towards Inishkeel Island, while Swan Mount provided a backdrop. By June 1905, Cannon had added further bedrooms. The facilities at this time included a darkroom for amateur photographers, a billiard and concert room, and a bell system which even extended to the roof garden.

There were several meetings held in the locality which campaigned to have the railway extended to Portnoo, but this never happened. Cannon died in 1919 and is buried in the old graveyard at Glenties. The hotel was closed for five years from 1920, probably due to Cannon's death. William Hemmersbach leased the business in 1925 and he would go on to run some of the better known hotels in the country. In 1939 the hotel was managed by a Mrs Sariah Nicholson (Cannon's daughter). During World War II or 'The Emergency' as it was known in neutral Ireland, the Portnoo Hotel continued to welcome visitors.

The notorious playwright Brendan Behan and his wife stayed at the Portnoo Hotel in 1960. It was subsequently bought by Joe Brennan, Minister for Labour and Social Welfare in 1973 and closed in 1982. The main building was partly demolished in 1994 and it is now in a ruinous state.

OPPOSITE PAGE Portnoo Hotel started life as a temperance hotel, attracting the followers of the Total Abstinence Association of the Sacred Heart.

LEFT AND ABOVE A roof garden allowed visitors to enjoy the extensive views to Narin Strand, Inishkeel Island and Swan Mount.

HOTEL. PORTNOO. NARIN Co. DONECAL 9778. W.L

GOLF HOTEL, PORTRUSH, ANTRIM
DEMOLISHED 2000

This striking hotel on the north coast of Antrim was built in the seaside town of Portrush in the 1880s between the railway line and the coast. Over the years the hotel had several name changes reflecting changing tastes in leisure and tourism. It was originally called the Hydropathic Hotel, in the period when water cures and hydrotherapy were in vogue. Hydrotherapy involved the use of water for the treatment of pain and injuries as well as for various mental health issues. The hotel was also conveniently located close to the Portrush golf links, which were established in 1888. Now called The Royal Portrush Golf Club, the course hosted the Open Championship, the oldest of golf's major championships, in 2019. The course is overlooked by the ruins of the 13th-century Dunluce Castle.

Towards the end of the 19th century the hotel changed its name to the Golf Hotel to reflect the growth in the sport and the stature of its local course.

In 1910 it was owned by a Miss McCrea. A picture postcard shows the cluttered drawing room of the hotel complete with a piano. Portrush offered the usual seaside attractions such as tea rooms, promenades, bandstands and ballrooms. Advertisements for the hotel highlighted the fact that it had direct access to sea bathing. Other nearby attractions included an ice-skating rink, and an amusement park called Barry's run by members of the Chipperfield Circus family.

The booming seaside town had as many as ten hotels, including a temperance hotel. A 1901 street directory stated that the permanent population of the town was about 1,800, but during the bathing season it increased to about 6,000. The 1911 census shows that the town was home to ten professional golfers, and a John Aitken was listed as a golf club maker. In 1892, Aitken was appointed club- and ball-maker (in those days an artisan skill) to the Royal Portrush Golf Club and he ran a shop at 10 Main Street. His clubs are now cherished collectors' items.

The town was the starting point for the world's first hydroelectric tram, which connected Portrush to the geological phenomenon and popular tourist attraction the Giant's Causeway. Run by the Giant's Causeway Tramway, the narrow-gauge service was the brainchild of the Irish engineer William Atcheson Traill. Two photos of different rolling stock on the tramway can be seen on page 12. The tracks passed close to the ruins of Dunluce Castle and the town of Bushmills. A rail route following the last two stops of the tramway was reintroduced in 2002.

During World War II, the hotel was occupied by the Department of Education. It then became a holiday home for young people, which was run by the Young People's Society of Christian Endeavor. This non-denominational Christian Evangelical group was founded in 1881 in the United States by Francis Edward Clark. In addition to prayer and bible studies, it also supported the temperance movement and had two other hotels in Ireland.

The hotel was demolished in the early 2000s, and in November 2019 planning was granted for the construction of twelve homes and eight apartment buildings on the site.

OPPOSITE PAGE It started life as the Hydropathic Hotel offering water cures and healthy sea air.

LEFT Conveniently situated for the railway station, it was even more convenient for one of Ireland's best golf courses.

SWIFTBROOK PAPER MILL, SAGGART, COUNTY DUBLIN

DEMOLISHED 2001

A vast paper mill complex was located in Saggart, in south-west County Dublin, and it was in operation from 1760 to 1972. Over its 200-year history it had four owners: the McDonnells, the Drurys, the Horsburghs and finally the Clondalkin Paper Mills.

Paper making is reliant upon access to large volumes of water. In 1836, John McDonnell diverted waters from the River Liffey to create an artificial branch, called the Camac. He used it to increase water pressure at the mill and to create additional mill ponds and mill races.

Early Ordnance Survey maps reveal the extent of the site and identify features such as weirs, sluices, mill ponds, mill houses, carpenters' workshops and weighbridges.

During the Famine the mill employed over 400 people. The large mill wheel was built by the Dublin firm of J. & R. Mallett in 1848 at their iron foundry near Parnell Street in the city. This large mill wheel became a tourist attraction and it was purported to turn 18 tonnes of water per minute.

A report on the mill published in 1911 outlines the way in which the three-storey rag house was divided according to the tasks required: the first floor housed uncleaned and unsorted rags upon delivery, the second floor was used for sorting, and the third for cleaning. The article was keen to stress that the air was circulated in order to protect the staff from the diseases that were thought to linger in clothing and rags.

In 1916, the mill produced the paper upon which the Irish Proclamation was printed. It had been purchased by the republican and socialist leader James Connolly for his journal *The Workers' Republic*. In the early decades of independent Ireland, paper from this mill was used for bank notes, stamps and high-grade writing paper. The paper for the Irish Sweepstakes tickets was also produced at Swiftbrook. The 'Ancient Irish Vellum' brand of notepaper was particularly popular and it was watermarked with traditional Irish symbols of the round tower and the Irish wolfhound. The mill closed for a short period in 1948 due to the lack of orders from Britain, which was still in recovery from World War II, but closed for good in 1972.

Most of the buildings on the site were demolished in 2001. Local residents have lobbied for the conservation of the last remaining structures – the paper mill's chimney and rag house – in an effort to salvage what is left of this early piece of Irish industrial heritage.

OPPOSITE PAGE Power was generated by the giant 1848 water wheel, the largest in Ireland.

RIGHT From rags to paper riches – the finished product being rolled out.

BELOW The mill was a significant employer in Saggart, Rathcoole, Newcastle and Brittas.

NAAS BARRACKS, COUNTY KILDARE

DEMOLISHED 2002

The barracks at Naas was built for local militias and opened in 1813. Its construction had commenced in 1810 at a prominent position in the middle of the town and it could accommodate eighteen officers and three hundred privates with the capacity for more in times of trouble. Over the years of British rule, many regiments were based at the barracks, including the Royal Madras Fusiliers and the Royal Bombay Fusiliers. In later years it was also a training depot for the Royal Dublin Fusiliers, the county regiment of Dublin, Kildare and Wicklow.

The barracks was designed to a template replicated throughout the British Empire and this included a series of quadrangles or squares upon which the soldiers drilled, as well as ancillary buildings fulfilling functions like the quartermasters store, stables and messes. The architects were Bernell, Browning and Behan.

The county of Kildare, in which Naas is located, played an integral part in Britain's military presence in Ireland. In addition to the Curragh camp, which housed no less than seven barracks, there were also barracks at Naas and Kildare town. It was estimated that approximately 20,000 troops were stationed in the county. A garden fête that took place at the barracks on the 8th of September 1916 typified the type of social engagement that centred around the barracks in spite of the recent Rising in Dublin and the ongoing global conflict. The day-long event included a concert from the band of the Royal Dublin Fusiliers, conjurors, a lawn tennis tournament, and a refreshment buffet and tea in the gymnasium. All proceeds were to be used to send food parcels to prisoners of war and to men fighting at the front.

During the early stages of World War I there was a rush to enlist, and many Naas businesses benefited from the influx of men waiting to sign up, especially after the German sinking of the Cunard liner RMS *Lusitania* in 1915. Recruitment in Kildare exceeded the national average.

A British presence was maintained during the War of Independence; however, the final troops left the barracks in February 1922. It was reported that a ceremony to mark the occasion could not happen within the barracks as the flagpole had been taken down by the departing army. Instead the tricolour was hoisted on a temporary pole beside the main gate.

The barracks was only occupied by the Irish Free State for a short time, between 1922 and 1928. It was announced in 1937 that the barracks was to become a slipper factory which hoped to employ sixty people. This factory was part of a national drive to make Ireland less reliant on imported goods. Following the closure of the factory it was again returned to military use, albeit as the Irish Army Apprentice School. This school was established in order to address the dearth of skilled craftsmen in the Irish Army.

The barracks was officially renamed as the Devoy Barracks in 1956 in honour of John Devoy, the Fenian leader who was born near Naas in 1842. The barracks was decommissioned in 1998 and several attempts were made to sell the fourteen-acre site, but it was eventually demolished. All that now remains of this impressive complex is the arch and clock tower.

OPPOSITE PAGE The barracks dated to 1810. In 1881 the 1st and 2nd Batallions of the Royal Dublin Fusiliers were formed from units of the Indian Army, while the Dublin County Militia became the 3rd, 4th and 5th Batallions.

LEFT The arch and clock tower, left of centre in this photo, remain standing.

THE BARRACKS, NAAS, Co. KILDARE 8211 W.L.

TILLIE AND HENDERSON SHIRT FACTORY, DERRY

DEMOLISHED 2003

Tillie and Henderson was one of many establishments in Derry that manufactured shirts for the international market. William Tillie's connection with the city began when the Scottish manufacturer came to Derry in 1850 to have shirts finished by outworkers. He later paired with fellow Scot John Henderson to establish a factory in the city. The tradition of shirt making in Derry had already been established by the mid 19th century with women working from their homes under the supervision of managers who called out to assess their work.

Initially Tillie and Henderson was based at a factory on Great St. James Street. However, they commissioned architect John Guy Ferguson to build them a much larger manufacturing base on Foyle Road, which was opened in 1856. At 19,000 square feet (1,765 square metres) it was the largest factory in Derry.

By the end of the 19th century there were twenty-seven factories in the city and by 1860 the payroll had risen from 450 to 800 people. The company were one of the first to introduce the sewing machine to the shirt-manufacturing industry; they also produced underclothes and the stiff detachable shirt collars and cuffs worn by men at the time.

The five-storey building was located on a riverside site covering nearly an acre. Significantly, more than three thousand outworkers from the surrounding counties were also employed in the production process. Such was the scale of the industry that it was referenced by Karl Marx in his book *Das Kapital*. His daughter Eleanor Aveling spoke at several meetings in the city in 1891.

The majority of workers were women and in the absence of any large industry offering employment to men in the city, women became the main breadwinners for many families in Derry. Indeed the workers were one of the first groups of Irish females to become unionized and over the years there were many conflicts between employer and employees.

Employment at the factory peaked at 4,500. In the late 1930s, the factory won contracts to supply shirts to branches of the military; however cheap imports from the Far East eventually led to reduced demand for their products.

In the 1970s the company moved out of their premises on Foyle Road and the site was abandoned. Plans were made to convert it into a museum and hotel; however, it was damaged by arson in 2002 and demolished in January 2003.

OPPOSITE PAGE, RIGHT AND ABOVE Three Bert Hardy images from November 1955. They were taken for a *Picture Post* feature titled 'One Man in Five is Out of Work'.

FERBANE POWER STATION, COUNTY OFFALY

DEMOLISHED 2003

Construction of this peat-burning power station began in 1953 and it took over two years to build. The fuel used to generate the electricity was local milled peat which had a moisture content of about 55 per cent. It was the first peat plant to be built outside of Russia and part of the Irish government's plan to exploit the nation's limited natural resources. It reached peak production in the 1970s and 1980s when it burned 2,000 tonnes of peat on a daily basis. It was one of six electricity stations run on peat which at one stage provided 40 per cent of Ireland's electricity needs.

Its two 262-foot-high (80-metre) cooling towers were made from reinforced concrete and the structures were visible for miles amid the flat midlands landscape. The use of peat was part of a policy which aimed to make Ireland self-sufficient in its generation of electricity. Eventually the hope was to become less reliant upon a single source of fuel.

Ferbane Power Station ceased production in 1999. The closure of the station was lamented by local people as the area was heavily dependent upon the plant for employment. It had been hoped that the cooling towers might be preserved as some kind of tourist attraction, combining viewing platforms with a museum, though this plan was never enacted. The spectacular demolition of Cooling Tower No.1 took place in December 1999 and it took less than three seconds to fall. The second tower went in 2002.

The industrial harvesting of the peatlands over the years had thrown up some astounding archaeological finds. Because of their waterlogged, anaerobic environment, bogs preserve organic materials, and Iron Age bog bodies (thought to be the victims of ritual sacrifice) have been unearthed in remarkable states of preservation. In 2006, an 8th-century vellum book of psalms called the Faddan More Psalter was found almost intact by the driver of a mechanical digger.

Material and scrappage from the power plant have been used by artists to make sculptures in the nearby Lough Boora Park, which is located amid 2,000 hectares (4,942 acres) of cutaway boglands. Parts of the towers were salvaged, including the steel tipplers (used to empty the wagons of peat as they

were delivered from the bog to the station) which are now used as burrow shelters in the park. The rest of the Ferbane complex was demolished between 2000 and 2003.

A neighbouring power station at Shannonbridge will close at the end of 2020 and this is indicative of a move away from fossil fuels towards more sustainable energy sources. The government's aim is to stop harvesting peat by 2030. In addition to greenhouse gas emissions, the bogs from which the peat was taken were unique biodiverse environments which were destroyed by the mechanical harvesting.

ABOVE A railway track was used for machine access to the peat around Ferbane.

OPPOSITE PAGE The power station pictured in 2002.

ABOVE Stones from the remnants of nearby Kilcolgan Castle were used to make the foundations for the power station.

THE TEMPLE. CASTLEBLAYNEY. CO. MONAGHAN. 9002. W.L.

Built for the Blayney family, this small summer house was located in the grounds of the family's County Monaghan estate near to Muckno Lake. Summer houses, or garden temples such as this one, often referenced the architecture of temples that young men of aristocratic families encountered upon their Grand Tours of Greek and Roman antiquities. Dating from the 1840s, the neoclassical temple was lit by tall rounded windows and included a portico set behind two Doric columns. These buildings were status symbols projecting both the owners' intellectualism and their leisured lifestyles and were often used for parties or musical events.

Robert Woodgate, an architect associated with Sir John Soane in London, designed the Blayney family's main house in a neoclassical style in 1799. The landscaped gardens were augmented by William Sawrey Gilpin in 1830. Gilpin's other Irish works included terraces for Caledon House in County Tyrone and landscaping for Crom Castle, County Fermanagh. He was the nephew of a more famous William Gilpin whose notions of the picturesque were influential in landscape design.

The estate at Castleblayney had previously been landscaped in what was known as the 'natural style', which sought to work with existing natural beauty and create vistas of Muckno Lake. The demesne surrounding the estate included features such as icehouses and ornamental gate-lodges. The temple was positioned on an elevated site set amid a wooded landscape with views of the lake.

Henry Thomas Hope, from the wealthy London banking family, purchased the estate from the last Lord Blayney in 1853. He did this through the Encumbered Estates Act Court, which facilitated the sale of estates whose owners could no longer meet their obligations. Accordingly, the house on the estate is known as both Hope and Blayney Castle. During this period Hope renovated the main house, doubling its size, adding a conservatory and placing the family crest on the house's facade.

It was also home to the Duke of Connaught (son of Queen Victoria) between 1900 and 1904 while he was the Commander in Chief of Forces in Ireland. The

family left the house in 1916 and a substantial sale of its contents, consisting of 1,400 lots, took place in 1926. The house was subsequently put to a number of uses: it functioned as Monaghan County Hospital between 1932 and 1937 and it was also owned by a Franciscan order of nuns in the mid 1940s.

A survey of the area taken in 2007 revealed that only one side of the temple remained. The main house was acquired by Monaghan County Council in the 1980s; it was destroyed in an arson attack in October 2010. The sorry fate of the house and temple follows a very similar trajectory to many of the 'Big Houses' of Ireland. Only the landscaped aspects of the demesne lands remain and these could perhaps be developed for recreational use.

OPPOSITE PAGE The Temple complete with manicured ivy in the late Victorian period.

ABOVE Although the grounds had previously been landscaped in the 'natural style', a century of neglect has given nature too strong a hold on the summer house.

LANSDOWNE ROAD STADIUM, DUBLIN
DEMOLISHED 2007

Close to the Dodder River and visible from the DART light railway, this stadium was credited with being the spiritual home of Irish rugby. Located in a South Dublin suburb, the original stadium was the brainchild of Henry Dunlop, who had founded the Irish Champion Athletic Club in 1871. He moved the club's activities from Trinity College Dublin to this new site outside the city centre. At first, the activities that took place at Lansdowne included croquet, archery, cricket and tennis, but the venue eventually became associated with rugby.

It was home to two rugby union teams: Lansdowne Football Club and Wanderers Football Club. International soccer matches were also played at the stadium from 1900 onwards, while athletics events were held there up until the 1950s. The first international rugby fixture at Lansdowne Road took place on the 11th of March 1878, and Ireland's opponents on this occasion were England.

After World War I, members of the two rugby clubs, many of whom had volunteered for the 7th Royal Dublin Fusiliers and seen action at Suvla Bay, set to work expanding the ground. They reclaimed land from the nearby Dodder River, which allowed for the creation of two back pitches and the reconfiguration of the main pitch in the direction it is today.

Irish international rugby matches were shared with Ravenhill Stadium, but after the upper west stand, which seated 8,000, was completed in 1954, the decision was taken to play all internationals at Lansdowne Road.

Over the years there were many additions and alterations to the original stadium, including the demolition of the old west lower stand in 1977. For many years it was felt that the old stadium was not fit for purpose and a new one was built between 2007 and 2010. The new stadium was the result of a collaboration between the IRFU and the soccer body the Football Association of Ireland (FAI). Government funding of €190 million was given to the project. Its architects were HOK Sports Architecture (now called Populous) in conjunction with Scott Tallon Walker. To the dismay of many, the naming rights were sold and the stadium is now known as the Aviva Stadium, after the multinational insurance company who sponsored it. The 50,000-seater stadium opened in 2010. A memorial to the IRFU members, including those from the 7th Royal Dublin Fusiliers, who fell in World War I has been transferred to the new stadium.

OPPOSITE PAGE An aerial view from the 1960s highlights the irregular shape of each terraced end to Lansdowne Road.

RIGHT The grandstand was extended over the railway line to increase capacity.

BELOW Little had changed when this photo was taken in 1999. Irish soccer internationals could not be played at Lansdowne Road due to a FIFA ruling that demanded all-seater stadiums.

BALLYMUN FLAT COMPLEX, DUBLIN
LAST TOWER FELL 2015

The Ballymun housing complex included seven landmark residential tower blocks built in a suburb on the north side of Dublin between 1966 and 1969. In contrast to much of post-war Europe, high-density, high-rise housing was not common in Ireland. In addition to the seven high-rise towers, the development also included lower flat complexes, which were either five or eight storeys, and more typical two-storey houses. Arthur and Swift were the architects and they were also responsible for other social housing projects such as St. Michael's Estate in Inchicore and Fingal County Council's headquarters on O'Connell Street.

The complex was built quickly to meet a housing crisis in the inner city where many people were living in unsuitable, overcrowded homes. Several house collapses had highlighted the dangerous conditions in which people were living and caused the Corporation to take emergency measures. The families who were moved to the new fifteen-storey blocks and other developments came from close-knit, well-established, inner-city communities where amenities such as shops, pubs and jobs were within walking distance. Few had cars and the lack of amenities sowed the seeds for future social problems. The promised landscaping and facilities, such as a cinema, were never delivered.

The photographs taken by Elinor Wiltshire in 1969, show a pristine and unsullied place, albeit a rather bare looking environment. The towers were named after the signatories of the Proclamation (Patrick Pearse, Thomas MacDonagh, Sean MacDermott, Eamonn Ceannt, Thomas Clarke, James Connolly and Joseph Plunkett), a document issued during the Rising of 1916, which outlined the leaders' vision for the country.

Unemployment in the 1980s and the hold of heroin addiction on Dublin's working-class communities further exacerbated the problems for Ballymun's residents. Negative media attention also meant that the area became synonymous with all that was wrong with the capital city and with high-rise living. The lack of maintenance of lifts and of shared spaces coupled with poor transport infrastructure were felt by some to be the crux of the area's problems rather than the high-rise nature of the development alone. Much of the media coverage failed to acknowledge the community cohesion that eventually grew in the area despite the lack of facilities.

A regeneration project commenced in the 2000s and provided new low-rise housing. The last of the tower blocks, Joseph Plunkett tower, was demolished in September 2015. The bulk of the regeneration was completed before the collapse of the Celtic Tiger and the economic recession; however, the proposed new shopping centre was not delivered. After several years of abandonment, the original shopping centre, the last of the original buildings, was demolished in 2019. A piece of public sculpture entitled *Misneach* (2010) by John Byrne celebrates Ballymun's tradition of horse ownership and shows a local teenager on horseback.

BELOW LEFT The towers have been referenced by many writers and musicians including U2 in their 1987 song *Running to Stand Still* from *The Joshua Tree* album and the 2004 film *Adam and Paul* (director Lenny Abrahamson).

OPPOSITE PAGE One of Elinor Wiltshire's classic photos from 1969 showing four girls from the estate and the excitement of hope and a new start in a modern environment.

BOTTOM Demolition in progress in 2007.

CLERYS DEPARTMENT STORE, DUBLIN
CLOSED 2015

Clerys department store was located on Dublin's main thoroughfare, Sackville (later O'Connell) Street. There was a rise in the prospects and aspirations of the Catholic middle classes in the mid 19th century who now had the leisure time and disposable income to shop in department stores.

Established in 1853, it was initially called 'The New Palatial Market' and was run by Mac Swiney, Delany and Co. However, Limerick-born M. J. Clery took over the business in 1896. During this period, staff lived in and underwent lengthy apprenticeships. The Imperial Hotel also operated from the upper floors of the building.

The original building was destroyed during the Easter Rising in 1916. The managers of the department store reacted quickly and moved business to their warehouses on Abbey Street, where they remained for six years until a new building opened in 1922. This new building was designed by Ashlin & Coleman and was modelled on Selfridges of London. The English-born architect who worked on its design, Robert Atkinson,

had previously collaborated with the Chicago architect Daniel H. Burnham. The new Clerys was five storeys tall and had six bronze-framed display windows which were the focal point for window shopping. The new store was a mixture of neoclassical design achieved with modern technology in the form of the building's reinforced concrete frame. The facade was of Portland stone and the store had a grand marble central staircase and a sunlit central space.

It boasted a ballroom that could hold five hundred people and a full orchestra. During this period, the store employed 1,000 staff and had forty-two separate counters.

The onset of World War II hit trade hard, however, and the store went into receivership. It was bought in 1941 by Denis Guiney who also owned bargain shops on nearby Talbot Street. He ran the store until his death in 1967 and his widow, Mary Leahy, continued to head the company until her death in 2004, aged 103.

Clerys clock, which hung over the main doors to the store, was a landmark, and meeting under Clerys clock was a tradition for Dublin couples. The original was made by Stokes of Cork. A new one was put in place in 1990.

Despite a radical upgrade in the 2000s, Clerys declined during the recession and saw a younger generation move to online shopping. It went into receivership again in 2012 and it closed its doors for the final time in 2015.

OPPOSITE PAGE Clerys in 2013 shortly before it closed.

BELOW LEFT The "Dublin Selfridges" opened in 1922.

BELOW Clerys' famous clock was a rendezvous point for almost a century.

ST. KEVIN'S HOSPITAL, CORK
DESTROYED BY FIRE 2017

St. Kevin's Hospital in Cork was a large, imposing building which housed a mental health institution. Positioned on an elevated site overlooking the River Lee about 1.5 miles (2.5 kilometres) to the west of the city, it was opened in 1899 as a nearby annexe to another earlier hospital known as the Eglinton Asylum (later the Cork District Asylum and, from 1952, Our Lady's Hospital).

Lunatic asylums, as they were originally called, were established in Ireland in the early 19th century under the Lunacy (Ireland) Act of 1821. The Eglinton, the second asylum built in Ireland, was originally a private institution.

The first building on the Eglinton site was designed by William Atkins and constructed between 1847 and 1852. Initially it consisted of three buildings: separate male and female hospitals and an administration block. These were joined together, making a long imposing Gothic facade.

The main building – now known as Atkins Hall – was built in limestone, and its Tudor-style windows were surrounded by fine stone carving. Patients were detained on an involuntary basis, often upon the word of their families and one doctor. There were particularly high levels of incarceration among single people who may have been deemed as superfluous to the family unit. An early annual report into the asylum showed that there were 226 admissions in 1855, and among those, eighty-six patients 'recovered', while sixty-five died.

St. Kevin's was a forbidding, red-brick, prison-like building to the east of Eglinton Hall which could accommodate up to five hundred patients. The institution was designed by Cork-born architect William Henry Hill. (Nearly all of the other buildings designed by Hill were in Cork and he appears to have specialized in churches and schools.)

The social policy of removing residents from large institutions – which began in the 1960s and peaked in the 1980s – meant that such large hospitals were no longer required. However, Our Lady's Hospital continued to care for residents until 1992 and St. Kevin's finally closed in 2002. Our Lady's was converted into apartments and renamed Atkins Hall after the original

architect of the building.

Despite the substantial money that was spent on security for the vulnerable empty property, St. Kevin's was badly damaged by fire on the evening of the 4th of June 2017. The fourteen-acre site, complete with derelict building, was put on the open market in 2018. The fate of such buildings hangs in the balance: some sites, such as St. Brendan's in Grangegorman, Dublin, which once housed two thousand patients, have been given over to educational use, while others lie in ruin.

OPPOSITE PAGE An aerial view of the Eglinton Asylum site in the 1950s. The twin gable ends of St. Kevin's are visible in the top right corner of the photo, edging out of the frame.

ABOVE St. Kevin's with its distinctive red brick frontage photographed in 2011.

RIGHT A view of St. Kevin's from the River Lee below.

HECTOR GREY SHOPS, DUBLIN
BUILDING DEMOLISHED 2019

Hector Grey's shop in Dublin city centre was synonymous with bargains and novelty and known by many generations of Dubliners. Grey was born in Scotland in 1904 and moved to Dublin in 1928. His real name was Alex Scott and he initially started working as a tipster at the various racecourses in and around Dublin. Originally from a strict religious background, he changed his name to avoid upsetting his family who disapproved of his association with gambling.

He established a pitch outside the Woollen Mills near Dublin's Ha'penny Bridge, where he sold cheap goods from a market stall. Each Sunday morning he regaled punters with banter and salesmanship, drawing in the crowds. His method of selling was rather like an auction where he sold the goods to the highest bidder once he had established a crowd.

He continued to sell at this location long after his other shops were established. His shops at Liffey Street and Mary Street were in business for over fifty years, selling bric-a-brac, toys, novelty items, decorations and what he called 'fancy goods'. His shop fronts were bright and colourful and a loudspeaker system announced the various bargains and novelties that were awaiting inside.

The photographs below show crowds (mainly men) on a Dublin street engaged in window-shopping. They were taken for the Irish Folklore Commission by Maurice Curtin. His work is unusual within the context of the Commission as it examines urban life and contrasts it with Folklore's typical emphasis upon the rural.

The shop was particularly associated with Christmas, as it sold sparkling decorations and a wide variety of cheap toys, Christmas crackers and glittering cards. His goods were sourced cheaply from mainly Asian countries.

Grey had spent his youth on British merchant ships and that is when he began to purchase inexpensive tin toys made in Japan or China. He attended his first trade fair in China in 1939 and continued to import from that country thereafter. He maintained two passports – one British and one Irish – in order to allow him to travel between various jurisdictions in the Far East.

In 1977 he is purported to have sold over a million pounds worth of toys over the Christmas period. He regularly offered bargains on 'Back to School' items such as copybooks, school bags and pencils. He also ran a more profitable wholesale business from a warehouse on Fitzgibbon Street. The business was so successful that he had branches of his shop in Crumlin Shopping Centre as well as two locations in the city centre, and he employed more than a hundred people.

Hector Grey died in 1985 at the age of 83. His funeral cortege made a final call at the Ha'penny Bridge where his original pitch stood. The company was wound up in 2016. The block where Hector Grey's shop stood on Upper Liffey Street was demolished in 2019 to make way for a hotel.

OPPOSITE PAGE The Hector Grey shop in Mary Street photographed in the 1960s.

BELOW The name 'Hector Grey' belonged to a famous Australian jockey. Alex Scott used the name to avoid embarrassing his family when he started off as a tipster. Grey/Scott was a lifelong fan of the turf and would often travel to Aintree for the Grand National.

INDEX